DECLUTTER YOUR MIND

Achieve Mental Clarity and
Inner Peace through Mindful Decluttering
(2023 Guide for Beginners)

Ruby Tomlinson

Table Of Contents

Chapter 1: The Philosophy of Decluttering

What's going on in your head? What effect does it have on you?
Could it be that the way you feel has a lot to do with it?

- With the actual objects that surround you? Physical possessions are more than simply the things that surround you in your exterior surroundings, right? They are an outward expression of what is going on in your head. Your cell phone bills It's your laundry. Your cupboards and shelves are crammed with unneeded objects, some of which you may have forgotten you had.
  The sofas and chairs in the corner were stacked high with old papers, books, and periodicals. The non-essential stuff in your life that takes up so much room and space that they begin to seem like a weight that weighs you down.
  According to experts, the normal human mind is packed with mental clutter. They term it an "unbearable burden" that we all bear but are unaware of the direct connection it has with our external circumstances.
  We've become so used to the loud "chatter" in our heads that we accept it as usual. It is now "normal" to be stressed. It's "normal" to have more than a dozen anxious, stressful thoughts going through your mind at once. Our failure to order our ideas in our heads is manifesting outside, and if you pause to look—truly look—at your immediate surroundings, ask yourself this one question: How many of these things do you require?
  Many of the things we possess are, in reality,

unnecessary. You don't need the same shirt in different colors. You don't need ten pairs of pants if you only wear two, since they're your favorites. You don't need multiple books stacked on your shelf if you don't intend to read them again. Most individuals are drowning in their own mess and are unaware of it. The typical American household has 300,000 objects. In one area, there are piles of letters, mail, and periodicals, as well as paperwork and documents. Expired food in the fridge; closets bulging at the seams with clothing, some of which you may not have worn in over a year or have even forgotten about Old shoes, keepsakes, and memories from your youth, as well as things you've received but never utilized, Now, come on, be honest. Do you really need all of this? Makinglemonadeblog.com is the source of the image.

Understanding and Managing Clutter

your house is not the only item that may get cluttered. In reality, a busy mind and a messy house are synonymous. Clinging onto clutter, for example, is the same as clinging onto the past.

You find it difficult to let go of certain belongings, even though you know you should, because of the emotional value and memories associated with them. You don't always want to get rid of something since it was a gift, and you don't want to upset the other person's emotions. You know you're not going to utilize it, yet you keep it anyhow. Holding on to objects that are no longer useful to you will prevent you from progressing since you can't look forward if you're continually looking back. When your mind is cluttered, it is the same thing. You can't bring yourself to let go of the past; you keep having the same thoughts over and over, and you have a hard time letting go of particular memories that hurt, even when you know you should.

Physical clutter is much simpler to comprehend than mental clutter. We can see it with physical clutter. We all know that clutter refers to the mounds and stacks of useless stuff that accumulate around our homes. Mental clutter is a bit more difficult to describe. Have you ever experienced a day where you felt completely frazzled? Like your mind is being tugged in a million different ways, and you're fatigued from the sheer amount of energy you've used in expanding your thinking and digesting the ideas you've had? On any given day, the typical person has between 60,000 and 80,000 ideas going through their heads. That translates to around 2,500 to 3,300 thoughts every hour. Other experts estimate the figure is significantly lower, possibly 50,000 ideas every day. That's still a large quantity, and to make matters worse, more than half of your thoughts are harmful. Most of your thoughts are either worthless or insignificant, which means they are taking up all of that empty space in your head.

Our brain is dynamic and always moving, like a butterfly fluttering from one gorgeous flower to the next, never pausing long enough to rest. Thinking is such an instinctive activity that we are unaware of our ideas until they are big enough to catch our attention. We're utterly unaware that these ideas are taking up too much mental space, making it impossible to focus and concentrate, and are nothing more than a distraction, diverting our attention away from what we should be focused on

in our lives instead. The time and hours you waste thinking about needless ideas may be better spent doing something constructive that will get you closer to your objectives. A crowded mind takes up more of your attention and time than it should, distracting you from what is vital in life.
What exactly is a crowded mind? It is a thought that:

- has a perplexing thinking process

- Cannot maintain a calm, productive, and focused state of mind.

- That strives to maintain a pleasant attitude

- That fights to maintain happiness.

- That is full of negative ideas that do not contribute to your life or well-being.
is lacking in focus

- Excessive ruminating Obsession with what is beyond your control

- Is having difficulty letting go of negativity, bitterness, and fury?

- Can be readily affected by events, views, and criticism.

- External factors might easily distract you.

In sum, a busy mind leads to a bad attitude. The most hazardous aspect of a crowded brain is that it allows you to lose control. By allowing your ideas to determine what you should think and feel, you give up control of your life. You forget that you are the only one who has control over your life—not your mind or your ideas. When you give up and let your ideas dictate your destiny, when you no longer take responsibility for your thoughts and actions, it's a clear indication that something has to change if you want to make a positive difference in your life.

The Effects of Clutter on the Brain

If your brain were a computer, clutter would resemble having too many tabs open in the brain at the same time. It's jumbled and unorganized, making it difficult to concentrate on anything. Because there are so many ideas going through our heads at any one moment, whether they are negative or contradict each other, they begin to create issues. These ideas are partly to blame for the tension, worry, and sadness that so many people face today, without recognizing how mental clutter contributes to it. When your ideas start impacting you negatively, you have a serious issue. Negative emotions are a symptom that your mind is crowded. It begins with a single idea, one emotion, and before you realize it, you're falling down a very steep slope of sad feelings and don't know how to stop. Negativity puts your thoughts in a horrible place that you don't want them to be in, and it may swiftly rob you of any chance of pleasure.

Your brain is not meant to be pushed in so many different ways. Your mind must be ordered. At ease.

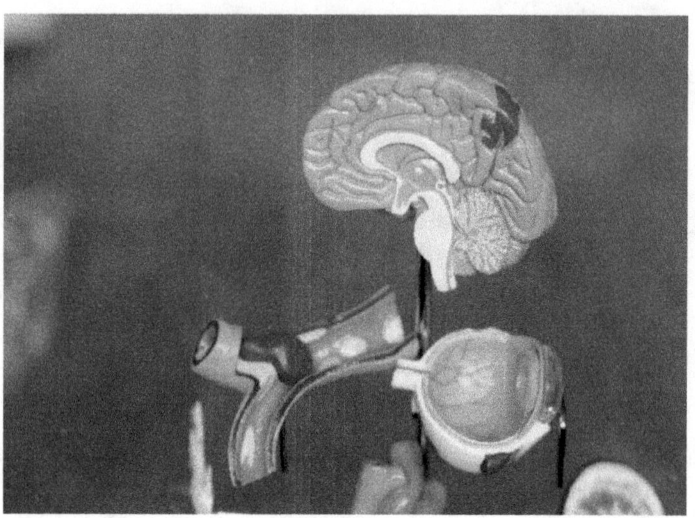

Concentrate on one thing at a time, ideally something pleasant and uplifting that makes you happy. The problem is that negativity cannot be completely avoided. There will be some less-than-pleasant times in life. It's much worse when we don't have the capacity to organize and filter the information we get. As an example, consider your email inbox. If you don't separate the vital emails from the trash mail, everything will build up into one giant mess, making your inbox too stressful to look at or even deal with. It would be a deception to suggest that we would never experience the stressful impacts of negativity.

We can't always avoid them, but you can learn how to analyze, appraise, and deal with them in better, healthier ways so they don't stay and clog your mind.

You are not attaining your maximum potential because of your mental patterns. Your "busy" mind is what causes you to feel "stuck", upset, nervous, and overwhelmed so quickly. Clutter is unhealthy for your brain, and the negativity it creates is one of the most crippling hindrances you can have, taking up so much mental space that there is no place for anything else. Don't forget about physical clutter, which is influencing you in the background without your knowledge. There's a saying that "mess equals stress," and there's a reason for it. Anyone who is surrounded by disarray finds it difficult to focus. We are so conditioned to a materialistic lifestyle that we assume our purchasing choices are based on serious consideration and solid rationale. We create excuses and provide justifications for why we need to buy more things. We make purchases in the hopes of becoming a happier version of ourselves, but when that doesn't happen, we become sad, and the emotions we experience just exacerbate the mental clutter that already exists.

What is NOT decluttering?

Decluttering is not only important but also enjoyable. It's freeing to feel as though a huge weight has been lifted off your shoulders. Your mind is not a run-down attic. It's not a location where you may dump your ideas in the hopes that they will either go away on their own or that you will forget about them. Emotions, dreams, aspirations, unmet wants, and old memories are all still there and will remain so until you discover a means to properly process and organize your thoughts. Doesn't it feel nice to get rid of all that unwanted trash when you spring-clean your home? That is exactly what you must accomplish with your thinking. Remove anything that isn't required and arrange what remains.

Confronting Your Emotions Is Mental Decluttering

Sweeping things under the rug will not work. That technique has never worked, and it will never work in the future. Avoidance and denial are two coping methods you should abandon since hiding your feelings will only lead to emotional and mental exhaustion.

Confronting your unwanted feelings may seem uncomfortable, but it is an essential aspect of the cleaning process.

Suppressing your emotions makes it difficult for your brain to think rationally.

Mental decluttering is not the same as completely avoiding worry.

Worry, like negativity, is difficult to avoid totally. There will be times when you worry; it is an unavoidable aspect of life. Mental decluttering is not about running away or denying and blocking out concern entirely, but being more proactive about it. Instead of allowing anxiety to consume your whole day, keep your thoughts structured by giving yourself time to worry before returning to your other activities. Choose a period that works best for you in between jobs and set aside 5 to 10 minutes for your problems.

There will always be something to be concerned about. Because you can't ignore concern forever, you've decided to be more proactive about it. Instead of allowing anxiety to consume your whole day, keep your thoughts structured by giving yourself time to worry before returning to your other activities. Reiterate your worries, but consider solutions rather than twisting your ideas and making yourself feel worse. Instead of circling the same concern over and over again, train your brain to be solution-oriented. This prevents your problems from spiraling out of control and distracting you throughout the day, allowing you to remain on top of all you need to accomplish while still processing your issues without abandoning them.

Tidying Up Your Environment Is What Mental Decluttering Is

The setting in which you spend the most of your time will have the greatest impact on your mind. It's not a good thing that we've become so used to our surroundings being chaotic, stressful, and cluttered that we no longer notice them. There's a fair possibility that at least one (if not many) areas of your house are crowded with too many things. How did it come to this point? For one thing, most of us these days are just too busy, running from one appointment to the next. We work long days at the office and are too fatigued to accomplish much else when we come home. Another factor is that cleaning is not an activity that many people like, and procrastinating and putting off cleaning the dirt around your house is how clutter accumulates. The larger the mess, the longer it will take you to clean it up. When the clutter has become much too large, a 5-minute cleaning will now take 2-3 hours to complete. Your house and mentality are both like ships on the sea. Keep piling junk in the boat, and it will ultimately sink under the weight of it all.

Mental decluttering is not restricted to material possessions.

Decluttering is more than just getting rid of unnecessary physical stuff around the house. Mental decluttering, in fact, involves all elements of your existence. Everything we are exposed to, everything we do, and everything we say or think has some effect on our braining, in fact, involves all elements of your existence. Everything we are exposed to, everything we do, and everything we say or think has some effect on our brain. Mental decluttering is getting rid of unhealthy relationships, outmoded beliefs, and undesirable behaviors. Anything that is bad in your surroundings must be removed. This includes any harmful people you may have in your life.

Can decluttering make a difference in your life?

It's difficult to start again when your past problems still have a grip on you. Every new year, most individuals begin with a list of passionately made new year goals. Motivation is strong, and we all plan to see our goals through to completion.

However, as the year progresses, the initial enthusiasm fades and we find ourselves drifting back into old routines. Slowly, your lack of drive seeps into other parts of your life. You can't seem to get anything done; your productivity is poor; you're easily distracted; you're exhausted all the time; you've lost your sense of purpose; and memories of the past haunt you. You'll be locked in this poisonous loop of thinking for the rest of your life if you don't clear your mind, squandering numerous years of your life feeling miserable.

Mental and physical decluttering can transform your life. Clutter is unneeded labor, and unnecessary work equals stress. Taking on more than you can manage is a burden, and when the mess becomes so terrible that you feel overwhelmed, there's only one thing to do: Set yourself free. Clutter is distracting and bothersome, and it contributes far too much negativity to our lives. Instead of fretting, it is time to become organized. Apart from the obvious advantages of having cleaner surroundings and a happier mind, decluttering is the answer you've been waiting for, and here's why it'll enhance your life:

More Space for What Really Matters: You create room in your life by purging the unneeded, both physical and emotional.

That gap allows you to regain your breath.

Accumulating tangible stuff makes it even more difficult for us to let go, and we sometimes cling on to things not because of the memories tied to them but because we constantly think, "What if I need this tomorrow, next week, or next year?" But be honest: how many times have you truly needed the stuff you're keeping "just in case"? You already have everything you need to exist and be happy, and you utilize it every day. You don't need it if you don't use it on a regular basis.

A Greater Sense of Happiness: Mental and physical decluttering provide you pleasure because you have a greater focus on what matters in life. You're more efficient, have greater concentration, and know what your priorities are. You find yourself enjoying life because you are no longer bound by the things that used to make you sad.

Rest of Mind: A loud mind can never be at rest. How could you be when your thoughts make you uneasy, concerned, or both? We cause a lot of stress for ourselves, and our connection to consumerism doesn't help things. Purchasing more items does not make us happy. Perhaps it does at the moment of purchase, but that sensation quickly goes. Materialism is nothing more than an attempt to fill an empty hole that we don't want to deal with, and once you accept this fact, it's much simpler to let go of everything that holds you back.

It Alters Your Thinking: If you continue to connect your happiness to external objects, it will be difficult to ever feel genuinely joyful. Decluttering your mind transforms the way you think, and you begin to discover satisfaction from within rather than depending on consumerism and trivial world items that never endure. When you have fewer distractions in your life, you will be able to redirect your attention to what actually matters. For example, your health, well-being, family, friends, partner, spouse, pets, hobbies, passion, and everything else will begin to take precedence in your life, and these are the things that you should value more than how many shiny new objects or clothes you were able to purchase.

Greater Efficiency: With a lot fewer things in your life, you suddenly find yourself being a lot more efficient than before. You can concentrate better, your priorities are more focused, and you feel lighter, happier, and able to work a lot more effectively and productively since there are fewer distractions around you. You'll find yourself managing your time more effectively with fewer distractions, and you won't feel as pressed as you used to. Because there is nothing to distract you from what you should be doing, you will be able to achieve more, feel more productive, and not feel as rushed for time as you formerly did.

Providing a Model for Future Generations Whether you have children now or in the future, living a basic, clutter-free, straightforward life will provide a positive example. You'll be teaching children essential life skills, such as how material items aren't responsible for happiness and how to be happy and appreciative for the things they currently have. It teaches kids to appreciate what they have more and to discriminate between necessities and desires.

Is it possible to become a more efficient learner through decluttering?

It certainly does. Distractions are the most significant productivity killers we face today. Even more so since we are always surrounded by the major source of distraction. Our cell phones They are also the source of a lot of the mental clutter we cope with. One of the numerous reasons that makes it difficult to concentrate long enough to acquire a new skill is social media. So it stands to reason that in order to improve productivity and our capacity for learning, we must reduce the distractions that make it difficult to do so.

Learning gets simpler when you have a defined life goal and no extraneous distractions stealing your concentration. With less mental junk dragging down your head, neuroplasticity can take place. Neuroplasticity is the root of all learning, yet it also results in an incredibly durable brain. Neuroplasticity is the capacity of your brain to alter its physical structure and function as a result of life events, thoughts, emotions, and recurrent actions. Because of this capacity, everything we do on a daily basis, whether good or bad, is wired into our system and the structure of our brain. One of the most challenging things we can do is learn to manage our thoughts. It's easy to let our ideas get the better of us, which is why negativity and external situations can have such a big impact on us. Do you want to live a better life? Begin by getting rid of everything that is harmful to your brain.

How should you begin decluttering?

When you have so many thoughts racing through your mind that you can't think straight, it's time to declutter. Consider the last time you cleaned your house or workstation and how you felt afterwards. How adjusting your exterior surroundings made it seem so much simpler to think? With fewer distractions, it became simpler to feel calmer, more focused, and so more productive. It is now just as necessary to do the same for your mental health. We are more distracted as a culture than we have ever been. It's getting more difficult to concentrate, and we're not finding the satisfaction or pleasure we desire.

To meet this need, minimalism has grown in popularity. The creators of "The Minimalists," Joshua Fields Millburn and Ryan Nicodemus, characterize this notion as "a tool to rid yourself of life's excess for focusing on what's important—so you can find happiness, fulfillment, and freedom." But what many people fail to realize is that it is far simpler to get rid of physical clutter than it is to get rid of mental clutter. Nobody wants to wake up in the morning feeling mentally burdened. Nobody enjoys dealing with self-doubt, fear, or negativity. Nobody gets out of bed in the morning thinking, "I want to feel stressed or overthink today." The ideas that trigger these bad feelings come and go, but when they do, they create unnecessary clutter in the mind. The problem is that you can never stop your thoughts. At the very least, not completely. A brain is an active machine that will continue to think for as long as we live. Thoughts will come and go as long as we have the capacity to think, so the issue is, what can we do to free up some mental space? How can we reduce the extra trash in our thinking?

This is accomplished in three steps:

Step 1: Revise the Story When you feel nervous, agitated, or overwhelmed, it's a sign that you're not thinking minimally at the time. The majority of our tension is caused by the stories we let ourselves construct in our minds, not by reality. It's the stories we tell ourselves about our reality that get us worked up, so the next time you feel this way, halt and write down what you're thinking. Each and every one of them Write down why you're irritated or concerned, what sparked those feelings, who or what led you to feel this way, what you're concerned about, and why you believe the conclusion will be unpleasant. Write down whatever you're thinking, capturing all your ideas on paper so you can see the kind of tale that's playing out in your head very clearly.

Don't filter it; just write it, regardless of how horrible you think it sounds. When you're finished and can't think of anything more to write, go back over your whole story and start crossing out anything that isn't based on facts using a red pen. Ask yourself, "What do I know to be true?" and strike out everything that is not founded on facts.

Here's an example of how this may appear: You're at work, and you're anxious because your boss just phoned to see how you're doing on a project you're hurrying to finish. "My boss is a micromanager," you think to yourself. He's calling to see how I'm doing. He's unhappy with my job, which is why he's doing this. He's going to fire me from the project for missing the deadline." When you start taking off everything that is not based on facts, you may end up with something like this: "My boss called to check on the project." "I'm running late for my deadline." See how the extra ideas are eliminated, leaving you with just two that are founded on facts? The facts will be accurate and should not generate undue dread or concern. When you start concentrating on the facts, it becomes evident what you should do next. In this case, you're falling behind on your project, so what can you do to catch up?

Resist jumping to conclusions. When something bad occurs to you, resist drawing conclusions and making predictions about what the future may hold. If something occurs and your first instinct is to imagine what a catastrophe it is and how it may all go wrong, it's an indicator that you're not thinking properly. When you begin to pile on the assumptions, tension begins to set in and your thinking gets hazier. To organize your thoughts, take out a piece of paper and draw two columns on it. Write down what occurred in one column. For example, a coworker who strolled straight by you without saying hi that occurs all the time; they may be busy or distracted, so the occurrence should not generate extra tension since there is a perfectly reasonable explanation for it.

Now, in the second column, put down your assumptions or conclusions as a consequence of that experience.

Make a note of any thoughts you have, such as "That colleague was disrespectful. That individual may be upset with me. Is it anything I said or did? Why didn't they acknowledge me? Do they no longer like me? I'm irritated because they didn't stop to say hi. That colleague has been so arrogant since they obtained that promotion." If you believe all of the assumptions you **just typed down,** you will rapidly get overwhelmed.

Your mind will tell you that the colleague dislikes you, even if this is not the case. You'll have to return to concentrating on what is founded on facts once again. If a concept lacks factual support, you should discard it before it produces excessive clutter in your mind.

Journaling Consciously: You may conduct this exercise using a pen or a notepad, and what you want to do is write without censoring all of your ideas at the moment.

This is known as aware journaling. It's similar to a brain dump in that you open the floodgates of your mind and allow a torrent of ideas to flow out onto paper. The process of putting your ideas into words slows your brain down enough to allow you to write them down. It's simpler to go on and forget about them once they're out of your thoughts. It's almost as if you've given them an outlet, and your brain is now free to go on to something else, leaving those ideas on paper. You don't have to review these ideas right away, either. Close your notepad or collect your papers and set them away before continuing with your routine.

- ## **What Comes Next?**

  Understanding why it's so vital to maintain your thoughts and surroundings Clutter-free is the only way to push yourself to persist with this practice over the long haul. Decluttering, both physically and psychologically, is a process that must be repeated as often as possible so that the clutter does not collect to the point where it becomes troublesome. The worry generated by a cluttered environment may ultimately lead to more significant mental health difficulties, which is just not worth it. It isn't worth losing your happiness for. Make it a goal for yourself to clear your thoughts one step at a time. Every day, a little bit more. Make a regimen for yourself until regular decluttering becomes a habit. Be open to adapting and modifying as you go, and be adaptable to the adjustments you must make. Above all, be dedicated to the decluttering process.

  Don't Keep It, Toss It: If you haven't utilized it in the last six months to a year, it's time to let it go. In this scenario, less is more. If you need something for a one-time event, borrow it. Stop the clutter from building up in your house by simply keeping the necessities you need to live and be happy. Purging on a regular basis entails checking in and assessing your surroundings. Things may accumulate without your knowledge, particularly clothes, so purging on a regular basis, perhaps twice a year, is beneficial. Mental decluttering may be done much more often by just checking in with yourself at least once a week and jotting down all your ideas. Keep in mind that having your emotions locked up inside is never a healthy thing.

Being Grateful: Most of us have more blessings than we can count. Unfortunately, our physical and mental clutter has caused us to lose sight of that face. As you concentrate on decluttering your thoughts and life one step at a time, you will quickly come to realize what is most important to you, and part of that process will be remembering to be thankful for all you have in your life. When you learn to appreciate what you already have, you will have fewer reasons to cling to what does not offer you joy.

Chapter 2: Building a Decluttering Mindset

Understanding is required to solve an issue. The only way to solve the problem once and for all is to identify the fundamental cause.

It is not sufficient to address just the apparent reasons. Every issue we deal with has an underlying core problem, and the only way to properly fix the problem in the long run is to address the issue at its root.

When we have a crowded mind, we must pause and ask ourselves why this is occurring. What is the core source of this notion that occupies so much mental space? Is this view justified or founded on truth? Take some time to consider if your concern is valid or irrational. If you notice that this idea (or a series of thoughts) continues to repeat itself, consider why and what the underlying cause is. Suppressing your feelings and thoughts will only make things worse for you since you are not addressing the main cause of the issue; you are just avoiding it for as long as possible, and the anxiety and concern will never go away.

Identifying mental clutter

what precisely is mental clutter? It's more than simply feeling like your mind is overflowing with thoughts and ideas that have nowhere to go. It's more than just a brain that is continually overthinking, pounding out one idea after another with no apparent breaks in between. Mental clutter is defined as:

The continual fear of what could or might not happen

Your previous regrets or missed chances that you wish you had taken when you had the opportunity

The never-ending list of things to accomplish that you're dreading or dreading

The unfinished business that continues to bother you, such as an email you forgot to send or debts you neglected to pay

being judgmental, grumbling, and engaging in other negative energy-inducing behaviors.

The drive to strive for perfection, establish unreasonable standards, and then be harsh on ourselves when we fail to meet those ideals

why do we have cluttered minds, and what causes them?

A crowded mind can never be fully at rest. When your thoughts are competing for your attention, it seems like a continual effort to be present and appreciate the experience. All it takes is one, two, or many thoughts to instantly transport you back in time or to ruminate on the future, neither of which is useful when both possibilities are beyond your control. This frame of mind does nothing except distract you from living in the moment and being totally dedicated to what you're meant to be doing right now. We have the ability to govern our ideas, rather than the other way around. Before we can achieve that, we must first understand why we have crowded thinking in the first place.

The only way to truly regain control of your mind for good is to achieve self-awareness by discovering the root cause of many of your unwanted ideas. Mental and emotional clutter may be just as toxic and detrimental as the physical clutter around us, if not more so. So, where does our mental congestion originate?

Excessive stress is becoming the leading cause of worry for many people. Anxiety is a common disorder in the United States, and the stress caused by information overload, too many choices, and physical clutter can lead to a variety of mental health issues such as overthinking, panic attacks, and depression due to the accumulation of mental clutter in the mind.

Feeling overburdened: Feeling overwhelmed by everything on your plate may exacerbate your worry and anxiety, resulting in all kinds of ideas that begin to pile up in your mind if there is no healthy way to channel them. When you have a lot to think about or worry about, knowing where to start might seem like a major challenge in and of itself. Even more so if you are under pressure to do everything on your own. It might be hard to wake up every day with so much to accomplish and not enough time to do it.

You Have Too Many Commitments. It's a typical issue among those who struggle to learn to say "no." You feel like the "bad guy" when you do, and you start thinking about what others will think of you if you say no. If you don't learn to maintain your ground, you'll be easily pushed about by individuals with more assertive personalities, and you'll constantly be at the mercy of someone else's agenda. It is impossible to satisfy everyone. It's just not feasible. You're terrified—you're terrified of facing what you can't control, and you're not alone. That is why so many people are concerned about the future, and not everyone is willing to make the required adjustments. Not everyone has the mental fortitude and courage to confront their concerns and not allow their anxieties overwhelm them to the point of paralysis. Your mind will always be fearful of what it cannot control or does not know, and until you learn to clear your mind of the useless clutter that fear creates, your thoughts will always have the upper hand in every scenario. You're Overburdened: Doing and even thinking too much may lead to emotional and mental exhaustion. It takes a lot of energy to process ideas virtually continuously from the moment you wake up. We're awake for many hours a day, which means the brain has a lot of work to perform, and a crowded mind consumes a lot more energy than a mind that is quiet, focused, and tranquil. Unfortunately, most of us these days are stretched too thin, balancing the obligations of both our work and personal lives, and if you don't allow yourself the time or space to think and properly process your ideas, it may rapidly seem like your brain is about to burst.

Poor Time Management: Procrastination is nearly always associated with poor time management. If you're guilty of leaving things until the last minute more frequently than you'd like to admit, it's likely that this is one of the many reasons you feel anxious and cognitively "blocked" at times. Because of all that mental clutter, you spend much too much time attempting to plan your answers rather than taking action. Your ideas have made you so worried that you're terrified of making errors, and that dread is beginning to hold you back. Mistakes are not always preventable; sometimes you have to try your best and hope that it is sufficient.

Perfectionists, in particular, suffer greatly from this. If we devote all of our effort to creating the ideal plan, there will be no time left to carry it through. Perfectionists might sometimes establish unattainable objectives for themselves, and then it strikes them hard if they fail to meet those goals due to the high degree of expectation they set for themselves. They open the door and welcome unwanted ideas into their heads, gradually making it feel crowded up there.

Negative Past Experiences: Making errors is how we learn. Everyone makes errors. The issue is that some individuals handle it better than others. Those that handle it effectively may learn from their errors, examine what went wrong and where they need to improve, and then move on to the next job at hand. Those who do not feel that they have made errors also entertain notions that undermine their confidence and self-esteem. The kinds of ideas that settle in your head and refuse to depart until you deliberately drive them out via the clearing process. You must focus on overcoming your fear of making mistakes like in the past. Any memories from the past that are still haunting you must be released.

Changes in Life: Not everyone adapts well to change and handles it effectively. Significant life transitions may create a lot of mental clutter if you don't have the mental and emotional skills you need to process and cope with the shift in a healthy manner. Some individuals find it difficult to face the changes that have occurred in their lives, and they begin to oppose these changes rather than embrace them. They cling to old habits that no longer serve them and allow irritation to rise when they discover their old methods are no longer effective.

The Physical Effects of Stress

Stress that is both chronic and extreme The second side effect of mental congestion is that we don't pay enough attention to it. Stress, as common as it is, is harmful to the body. There's a reason it's known as the silent killer. It may seem like a tough phrase, but it accurately describes what stress can do to you. It is a quiet killer because you do not see it until it is too late. Stress may arise from a variety of causes. It might be emotional, work-related, or even physical. It refers to how the human body reacts to requests or threats. Some stress may be beneficial, but being consistently stressed for extended periods of time can have a number of harmful impacts on the body. When you are under emotional, mental, or physical stress, your sympathetic nervous system sends a signal to your brain's hypothalamus, which governs our emotional reactions and the production of chemicals in the body. These same hormones are in charge of inducing the fight-or-flight response. While this reaction was originally intended to safeguard and prepare our bodies to respond rapidly in the event of an emergency, living in this state for extended periods of time may put you in danger of some serious health issues.

Here are some instances of what stress causes to the body: heightened rage

Abuse of substances such as cigarettes, narcotics, or alcohol, which are often used as crutches to cope with stress,

Eating too much or too little

There are fewer and fewer social contacts.

Additional arguments

Less physical activity

Isolating oneself from others Sleeping excessively or insufficiently Demotivated

Sense of humor declines

Depression

Moodiness

Irritability

Thinking about the worst-case scenario

Panic

Cynicism

Anxiety

Feeling overburdened

Frustration

Memory issues

Poor decision-making

unable to focus.

"Brain Fog"

Indecision
Self-doubt comes from starting many projects but accomplishing little.
When chronic stress manifests physically, it may cause the following medical problems:
Headaches
Heartburn
Breathing quickly
The risk of a heart attack has increased.
Depression has increased.
Insomnia
high heart rate
Fertility issues
Sexual dysfunction
Period omissions
Immune system weakness
High blood pressure and blood sugar levels
Aches and pains in the stomach
Reduced sexual desire
Muscle tensile tension

Stress is more than simply an emotion that you experience when you are under pressure or overwhelmed. This inbuilt physiologic reaction spreads throughout the body. Because of the harm it causes to the internal organs, our bodies were not designed to tolerate this basic fight-or-flight reaction for an extended period of time. Cortisol, adrenalin (epinephrine), and norepinephrine are stress hormones generated by the adrenal gland. Hormones flow via your circulation and reach your heart and blood vessels. Adrenaline causes your heart to beat quicker and boosts your blood pressure, eventually leading to hypertension. Cortisol also causes the endothelium (the inner lining of blood vessels) to malfunction. Clearly, persistent, chronic stress is bad for the body.

Mental Decluttering

Decluttering is a difficult task for many people. Even after cleaning and clearing your physical area, life might still seem hectic if your mental space is cluttered.

Mental space is a shambles. We don't spend enough time searching inward and draining out the negative to create a place for good. There will always be a lot of things coming in and out of your headspace, so develop a routine of mentally cleaning and getting rid of what you don't need to make room for the things that "spark joy," in the words of Marie Kondo. Negative and needless ideas will continue to make you unhappy, and most of the time we aren't even aware these thoughts are festering in our brains unless we actively practice mindfulness.

Mental decluttering will be emotional, even unpleasant, and tough. Decluttering the mind would be approached in the same way that you would declutter any physical place around you. To free up room, you must empty everything. Controlling the Data You Receive When you're on a diet, you think about what you eat and what you put into your body. You make certain that only healthful foods enter your body. This is precisely what you must do for your mind. To be conscious of the information you absorb and to avoid unneeded garbage.

For example, consider what you see on social media. That information isn't really useful, and it won't significantly enhance your life, yet we spend hours on these social media sites and allow ourselves to be influenced by what we see. Staying away from drama and anything over which you have no control is one method of managing the clutter in your head. It's nothing more than brain trash, and if the news isn't helping you, it's not worth paying attention to. Restore Balance in Your Life: The reason so many individuals are exhausted is because they continue to run. They rush from one location to the next, from one appointment to the next, from one job to the next, with no time in between to sit down, take a breather, and recharge. You're making far too many compromises, and it's taking a mental toll on you.

Understandably, there are instances when you must make these sacrifices and sprints in order to advance in life or go one step closer to your objective. But the key to regaining balance in your life is understanding when to run and when to take a breather and learning to take care of yourself first.

Reestablish Your Routine: When you're distracted by your thoughts and the mental diversions going on in your brain, it's easy for a routine to slip by the wayside. Lack of a routine may not seem like a major concern at first, but it really makes you less efficient in the long term. Our minds need order as well as a dependable system. A routine guarantees that you're making the most of your time, and when you get things done effectively, you're less stressed and don't feel like you're always chasing the clock or running out of time.

Create a morning and daily routine. This way, even if you have a lot to accomplish, you'll have a functional system that will allow you to do tasks in the most effective manner possible.

Have a Reliable System: Have a reliable system in place for receiving, processing, and storing information. This system should be something that works for you. Because everyone has their own method of doing things, what works for you may not work for someone else. You are having difficulty letting go of harmful ideas because you have not yet found a strategy that works for you. Or your existing strategy for controlling your thoughts is ineffective. A weekly review is an example of a trusted system. If you have the time to do this every day, that's fantastic; if not, once a week will be enough. Even 5 to 10 minutes each day for reflection is plenty to get started.

When our internal turmoil, ideas, and fears are imprisoned within our heads with no escape option, they might seem enlarged and potentially worse. In this situation, a frequent review or reflection process would be beneficial.

Say no when necessary. Your sentiments and emotions are just as important as anybody else's, and they should never be ignored. If saying yes would bring you more stress than you're prepared to bear, then say no and don't feel bad about it. Respect your emotions enough to set clear limits and say no to anything that will not make you happy. You owe it to yourself to prioritize your happiness right now, and it's time to get rid of the stressful junk that has been clogging your head for far too long. Make yourself happy first before attempting to make others happy.

The Pomodoro Method: In one of his works, Cyril Northcote Parkinson invented the term "Parkinson Law" in 1955. "Work expands to fill the time available for completion," he wrote. This suggests that the more time we set aside for completing a work or project, the longer it takes to do it. As a result, we often feel as though we are unable to accomplish a job, even when we believe we have allowed ourselves enough time to work on it. Finally, the best way to avoid this is to set stronger deadlines and drive yourself to meet them. This is where the "Pomodoro Technique" comes in. A guy named Francesco Cirillo pioneered this method in the late 1980s.

This is a time management approach that focuses on breaking down work into 25-minute increments. You will be given a 5-minute break after each 25-minute period. After completing four 25-minute intervals in a row, you are offered a longer break, which is normally between 15 and 30 minutes. Take advantage of these pauses to recharge and allow yourself some room to re-center and re-find your concentration. Use this time to unwind and clear your mind of anything that is upsetting you, so you can return to work refreshed and ready to concentrate.

Concentrate on life's priorities.

Who would have guessed that having more alternatives might be a disadvantage? The "Paradox of Choice" is a concept created by psychologist Barry Schwartz to describe how having too many options leads to increased feelings of unhappiness, anxiety, indecision, and immobility. It's almost as though freedom of choice were a two-edged sword. As much as we value our opportunity to pick the best route for us, having too many alternatives to cope with may be stressful. Having a lot more options is excellent and may result in objectively superior outcomes, but it is not a guarantee that you will be pleased. There will always be doubts about whether you made the proper decision, which will set off a new wave of anxious feelings.

As a result, defining your priorities is a vital ability to master in order to manage your thoughts and your time. As much as we would want to assign equal weight to all of the chores that must be completed, the fact is that we cannot. There is only so much time in the day, and in order to get the most of it, you must overcome the dilemma of choice by concentrating on what your priorities are. You must realize that you cannot accomplish everything and that this is perfectly OK. You can still do whatever you put your mind to if you manage your time effectively. Your life is divided into various categories:

Family, friendships, and connections are the most important things in life.

The Second Most Important Things: Your work, your home, and the vehicle that transports you from one location to another.

The Minor Stuff: everything else in your life that you need to accomplish in order to live and get through the day. For example, the errands you need to run and the appointments you need to keep

If you spend too much time worrying about little matters,

you won't have time for the major things that make you happy. When you start paying attention to the things that are important to your happiness, you will begin to live a happier life and have a clearer mind.

Setting your priorities and taking care of the vital things first will allow everything else to fall into place. You know what you should do, and the reason you're still failing is because you're not focused on your priorities. All of the background noise and mental clutter are distracting you. People fail to do what they know they should. It's no surprise that we spend so much of our time feeling dissatisfied and upset.

Today, more than ever, we need these priorities to help us use our time wisely and productively. With so much to accomplish, the last thing you want to do is waste time on projects or chores that don't add value to your life. Your most important resources are time and energy, and every instant you spend worrying is another moment you're squandering these precious resources that you will never get back. Making your life more satisfying is the easiest approach to starting to clean your mind from the anxieties that drag you down, and here is how you start concentrating on your priorities on a daily basis:

Define Urgency: These are the jobs that need your immediate attention and have urgent implications.

Define What Is Important: These are the tasks that will assist you in achieving your long-term objectives and values. The most critical chores will have the most influence on your life, but since they often have no clear deadline and the repercussions are not imminent, it is simpler to procrastinate on them.

You must create a to-do list every day. The items on the to-do list must be assigned to one of four categories on the Eisenhower Matrix. If you read Stephen Covey's The 7 Habits of Highly Effective People, you may have come across this word.

Covey discusses how the Eisenhower Matrix may help you rapidly identify the tasks that you need to concentrate on when you're short on time.

Important or Urgent: The first box of the matrix is for your critical and time-sensitive jobs with immediate implications. Medical emergency, for example, or project deadlines. The method for completing these activities is to accomplish them first and quickly.

Important/Not Urgent: The next box in the matrix includes items such as health, relationships, objectives, aspirations, and desires. The duties that are significant but not urgent The action step in this box is to arrange and select when to carry out the necessary tasks. Because they are still categorized as essential, you must respond as soon as possible, but you do not have to act immediately.

Urgent/Not Important: Items in this category might include unexpected phone calls, disruptions to your productivity, and emails. It is simple to identify the objects that belong in this group. They almost always include other people's priorities. If the tasks in this box do not immediately result in a consequence for you, delegate or postpone them to a later time.

Not urgent or important: The fourth and final box contains everything else in your life. Checking social media, watching TV, and other time-wasting activities that don't add significantly to your objectives

Items in this category are frequently attractive and difficult to reject since they require much less work. You have the option of doing it later or avoiding it totally.

You also need to complete the following: Choose whether to act or react. To act, you must be confident of what is essential to you and the outcomes you want. Without it, it's easy to become reactive and allow insignificant things to drive your thoughts and behaviors. Once you've determined your priorities, build your life around them. This gives your mind something to concentrate on, making it less inclined to consider the unwanted ideas that pass through it. Defining your priorities is the best way to focus on them and respect your time.

Determine Your Core Values

Do you realize who you are? If you had to choose three to five, what would they be?

What words would you choose to describe yourself? We believe we have we know who we are, yet it suddenly becomes difficult to express ourselves.

Doesn't it describe it when your head is crowded with confusion? What has been in charge of your life? What is the name of the invisible force?

Been the driving force behind the majority of your decisions? What exactly is this force?

Helps you determine what the best course of action is? Fundamental principles.

The concepts that govern and determine core values are characterized as Human activity and conduct. They assist you in distinguishing between the two.

Between what is good and bad, acting as a moral compass to guide you Make smarter judgments when necessary. Your fundamental principles are the basis on which your life is based, and if you envisioned what your core values seemed to be; envision yourself as a tree with the roots that hold you solid are your essential values. In the absence of these, it would be simple to get confused, dislodged, and unclear about what to do with roots. Worry, anxiety, and overthinking. When your values are clear, It is simpler to advocate for what you believe in, successfully pushing fight back against the negative and harmful ideas that attempt to overwhelm you Destroy your self-esteem. It is simpler to determine why.

You arrive at a certain choice, or why you chose to behave the way you do you do. Having a guiding philosophy offers you a feeling of direction, and it's beneficial. It's also easy to recall what your priorities are. They maintain you are committed to being the person you want to be. To live the life you've always wanted. When you live in accordance with your living by your basic beliefs and a set of objectives and priorities. Producing a mental environment conducive to serenity, tranquility, clarity, and, most importantly, Happiness for everybody. You need a sixth sense to recognize when anything is awry.

You have a good handle on what is best for you. The fundamental principles, the holy truths that determine who you are regardless of what occurs or what scenario you are in the situation you find yourself in will never change.

When you live in, you will have a happy and clutter-free mind. Accord with your basic principles. That is, your ideals must be consistent. Encouraging and pushing you to become the person you want to be. Core Values must exist. They must stand out and be memorable. Be significant. They must enhance every aspect of your life, beginning with the from the personal to the professional. If you haven't decided what yours is, aren't yet, that's OK. There will always be conflicts if essential ideals are not upheld.

Resistance. Life will always seem like it demands a lot more effort. Takes effort and energy simply to get anything done, which may be exhausting. This is what occurs in your life when you understand what your values are. You're less inclined to give in to peer pressure or make rash decisions.

You make better judgments and avoid those that are in contradiction with your values. Essential beliefs, resulting in sadness and a feeling of failure frustration. It reminds you to prioritize your expectations and requirements. It greatly simplifies the decision-making process. Process. If your choice or behavior is consistent with your values, then proceed.

do it. You don't do anything if it doesn't work. Simple. Creating the life you desire is not as difficult as it seems. Locate your fundamental principles and choose your priorities since they are the components that hold you together and keep you grounded. Especially at times of stress, when you need them the most. Your basic beliefs and priorities form a clear line in the sand what are you prepared to tolerate in your life? Anything that does not fit these parts, especially the unhelpful, must be removed. Thoughts that have no genuine purpose.

Chapter 3: Cleaning Up Your Space

We sometimes forget that living in a cluttered environment, Clutter, grime, and disorganization may all take their toll. There isn't nobody. There are some who will tell you that they like feeling overwhelmed. The phrase alone elicits discomfort, alienation, and failure. It's almost as though you're disappointed in yourself for not being able to cope. That's the term you'll be using a lot if you're a writer. Dwell in the habitat mentioned above. Stepping into you can't find anything you're searching for in your garage, and it's a mess. Battle to get around the boxes and heaps of material strewn all over the area. When you open your drawers, you find a lot of goods thrown in there you don't even use anymore. Performing a

A simple inventory of your house may reveal various things that surprise you. You have no recollection of purchasing. That's the issue with things. It tends to accumulate. And, if you're like so many others, it's difficult to let go. Feeling "overwhelmed" by the clutter in our life has become common. Become a well-known filthy little secret. The majority of us go through it, yet nobody wants to speak about it because talking about it implies you've done something wrong. You must accept that you have a clutter issue. This is something that many of us have.

We have a compulsive drive to fill whatever we have. We stuff our homes and our lives. Automobiles, offices, workstations, mobile phones, tablets, etc. We have laptops, storage containers, cabinets, and shelves, and we fill both of them. With unneeded clutter in our brains and souls. It's more than we can handle. It's no surprise that we're feeling overwhelmed. Why Do we keep taking more and more? Because we think that "more" is possible. Will result in contentment. We feel that if we get the most recent mobile phone, we're going to be pleased. If we purchase the most recent model on the market,

We're going to be pleased. A new watch, pants, shoes, and so on goods for the house. Advertisements and ads often depict a when we buy their goods or participate in their activities their assistance. Is it true that shopping makes us happy? On various occasions It does on some level, but it isn't the type of happiness that lasts long.

We continue to buy and gather, believing with each new acquisition.

that it will eventually make us happy. In truth, all it does is

keep the overpowering emotion we already have. The phrases

In today's world, the terms "clutter", "decluttering", and "minimalism" have proliferated.

Because this is a very serious issue in society. We are all aware that

Clutter is not restricted to the tangible items that clog up our homes.

It might be digital, mental, spiritual, or emotional space. The

When we think about clutter, our thoughts instantly wander to physical clutter.

hear the phrase "clutter" To address the remaining issues of a crowded existence,

You must focus on the physical, and the rest will follow.

place. When your life is simplified, your brain becomes more efficient.

It is less cluttered. Coming home to a clean, well-organized place

Having lots of space to walk about is a breath of fresh air after the

You left the loud outside world behind as you came through the front door.

door.

Your home is only a container.

We absolutely regard it as such. Yes, we must realize that our houses are not perfect.

You are a container. It's where we store everything we possess. What we have

What we need to learn now is how to halt the oversupply.

Messiness, no matter how slight, ultimately takes its toll. It might not.

seem to be a randomly dispersed tiny clump of objects here and there

surrounding your house will do significant harm, but every form

Your attention is drawn to the clutter. It may or may not be conscious.

Although you are paying attention, your brain is still processing these inputs.

whether or whether you're paying attention.

Your home is a container, and if you are not attentive, it will leak.

become a container that swiftly fills to the max. How do identify

if you have a significant clutter issue in your home?

By following this basic rule: If you need to relocate one,

You have a clutter issue if you have to move one object to get to another. You should not do so.

You must move things around to get to what you need.

Every item should be simply and rapidly accessible.

should have a "home" where everything has a place.

There's nothing wrong with having things, and decluttering isn't necessary.

That doesn't imply you have to get rid of more than half of your possessions.

Decluttering is keeping just what you need to be happy.

and not much else. That's all. You'll still have possessions; it's just that you'll have less of them.

The difference is that you'll have fewer things.

Your house is a container, and you happen to live in one.

When you're not at work, you should spend a lot of time there. If this is the case,

You'll notice that your brain is becoming progressively overburdened.

It will be difficult to concentrate and make judgments, and mental tiredness will set in.

leave you feeling fatigued and depleted of energy all the time. In

keeping up with this continual, on-the-go, and frantic pace

We have forgotten that there are other parts of our lives that we must consider.

that need attention. Our health, relationships, and personal development

and mental health have taken a back seat as we rush to see what else we can have.

We can purchase, find out who has what new goods, and discover reasons to buy.

We are continually making new and unneeded purchases that we do not require.

We have gotten way too consumeristic and materialistic, and it is beginning to show.

It's time to alter everything.

A house should be a place you look forward to returning to.

day. A place that makes you joyful, boosts your spirits, and elevates you.

your morale. It should be your refuge, not a source of stress.

Even more anxiety. You must do the following in order to build such an environment:

achieve two objectives:

Simplicity for Greater Clarity - Remove everything that is unnecessary.

That's the rule of thumb for keeping things simple. If you do not,

If you don't need it, chuck it (or donate it). Princeton University conducted one research.

According to research, cleaning up the atmosphere inside your home is beneficial.

Your immediate area of view may aid in preventing your brain from

overloading. It is much simpler to concentrate when there is no brain fog.

Consider your options carefully.

Escape Boredom - As much as we need regularity,

It might get tedious after a time. You will lose if this occurs.

motivation and the drive to get things done. The United States of America

According to the Psychological Association, the reason you feel

It's possible that you're bored because what you're doing now has no meaning.

In other words, there are stages in your everyday routine or surroundings.

They do not make you happy or contented. conducted research on

This topic implies that there has been a shift in your surroundings, even if it is little.

If it is just a tiny alteration, it may be all you need to modify your ways.

attitude and get a new perspective on life. If your office desk

is crowded and makes you feel unmotivated, cleaning everything away and starting again

Leaving nothing except your laptop and a notebook on it may be dangerous.

You will feel revitalized afterward. This is being processed by your brain as

Something fresh, and this excites me. It's been a long time.

because it saw an empty and simple desk, and that change

wakes up the brain, reinvigorating your feeling of purpose

at it.

Space Is More Important Than Stuff

Space is an underappreciated asset. We place a high priority on our

We have so many material possessions that we forget how much room we have.

There is only so much space in your house, vehicle, desk, garage, closet, and so on.

Before it's stuffed to the brim, drawers can handle it. But we can't.

We can't seem to get ourselves to quit shopping. There is no longer any such thing as space.

Considered "space" when there is no more room to move about.

Have you ever felt as though you didn't have enough space to breathe?

Claustrophobic? Trapped? Maybe confined? That is your mind.

attempting to alert you to the fact that there is much too much going on. Now, contrast

comparable sensations to how you feel after a little spring cleaning

cleaning. Do you let out a sigh of relief? Do you feel lighter right away?

Better? We may learn to cherish the valuable space we have if we learn how to respect it.

If we had, maybe we wouldn't be so eager to fill it up again as quickly.

because we've created some space.

The advantages of appreciating your space and decluttering go beyond attempting to save money.

to make your house appear like something out of a Pinterest board. It's the mental, physical, emotional, and even financial advantages that you will get

This is the benefit that makes the procedure worthwhile. Unsurprisingly, the

thought about getting rid of the majority of what you've gathered through the years

Years may be intimidating. Some individuals have very intense emotional responses.

connection to particular goods they own, even though they may not need them

I hadn't touched or utilized those products in years. The matter of

"What if I require this?""will always linger in the back of your mind."

mind. But consider this: Is the mess worth your stress?

Consider what it might be like to live in a totally automated house.

free of tension. to always know where you may get what you're looking for

need. No more being annoyed by misplaced goods. No longer

hours wasted looking everywhere for what you need (unfortunately, this

When you're in a rush, this always occurs). These are the modifications.

you go through will be felt from inside, and they are the

alterations that are much more potent than anything that occurs in your environment. Decluttering puts you straight back to the beginning.

what is most important by reminding you that you don't have to

depend on worldly possessions to feel contented and satisfied

Individual who is content. A productive lifestyle's kryptonite is stress.

Interestingly, one 2011 Princeton Neuroscience study

If you were having difficulty, the Institute revealed that clutter was the issue.

to concentrate on something without becoming sidetracked quickly. Essentially, the

The more stress and stimulus your brain is subjected to, the more

Concentration will be more difficult.

We're all fighting separate fights with clutter. Some of them are

Others may be more emotional or mental, while others may be more physical. But

You will notice the following as you begin to value your space.

Changes are taking place:

You have a greater sense of relief since you have cleared away the

Clutter in your life will seem like a huge weight has been lifted.

lifted from your shoulders. Suddenly, you have breathing space.

time and again. We often underestimate how much we are.

influenced by the accumulation of stuff and clutter around

us till we get rid of it and feel a lot better after we've done so a

couple stuff out.

You're Getting a Better Idea of What You Don't Want -

Working through your stuff meticulously can help you realize

which ones are the most important to you? gaining understanding of what

you don't want at the same time develops clarity about the things

You do desire. Decluttering seems to be an easy enough task.

in clarity, but the capacity to differentiate what you want from what you don't want

Things you don't desire will manifest themselves in other aspects of your life.

too.

You're Motivated Again - There's an extra advantage to being motivated.

capable of distinguishing between what you want and what you don't want. Your

Motivation has been reawakened as a result of the newly discovered, clearer

You have a reason to live. Without the extraneous distractions

By removing your concentration, you are able to observe your

Remember your objectives and what you want to achieve.

accomplish.

You are much more efficient - you can focus.

healthier, your priorities are more focused, and you are feeling

lighter, happier, and able to operate much more productively and effectively

Since you have more time, make better use of it

There are less distractions surrounding you.

Less stress equals better mental health - increased attention and concentration.

Clarity awakens you to what you have been ignoring all along.

That you are more valuable than any material goods you may have

Purchase is a possibility. When you begin to concentrate on yourself again,

Because you're happy, your mental and physical health improves.

Working on becoming a better version of yourself. If you carried on living with

Without the tension, none of this would be possible.

How Do I Get Rid of Clutter in My Home?
Getting Rid of Junk in Your Home

Let's be clear about one thing right now. The chances of you ever going

It is quite unlikely that you will ever need your "just in case" equipment. Be
Ask yourself how many times it has happened.

happened? Where you needed to reach for your "just in case" supplies

and said to yourself, "Wow! I'm so pleased I saved everything.

all of these years!" You are keeping these objects because of the

It has sentimental or emotional worth. These objects are important to you.

It's natural that you'd rather have memories than clutter.

Getting the Party Started

The process of getting rid of anything superfluous in your house is not easy.

It will not be simple, nor will it be fast. The majority of individuals are

They will encounter three major issues if they try to

For the first time, declutter:

They misjudge the amount of room the things need.

They are unconcerned about the expense of storing them.

They overestimate or overstate the likelihood of requiring

It will be used in the future.

A formula is required to overcome these hurdles. A distinguishing feature

In reality, it's a formula. The formula is divided into five steps:

Frequency: When was the last time you used the item?

The frequency with which you utilize the thing

Acquisition Cost: How costly or difficult it is to replace

Storage expenses: The expenses of upkeep or storage associated with

the thing

Cost of Retrieval: How much would it cost to store it?

to locate the thing when you want it? Is this item in danger of being stolen?

Are you becoming outmoded or out of date?

As a result, your formula is the FR3C formula shown above. To determine whether

If you believe the object is valuable, follow these steps:
LOW (Frequency, Regularity, and Acquisition) + HIGH
(Storage and Acquisition)
Not Worth Keeping Around (Retrieval)
Here is an example of the formula in action:
The last time you wore those shoes was two years ago.
recently (Low)
Regularity: You wore it just once or twice (low).
Acquisition: These are inexpensive and readily replaced.
(Low)
Storage: It's taking up needless closet space.
might be better used (high)
Retrieve: Two-year-old sneakers are most likely out of
date.
(High)
It's a bit more difficult to accomplish this with emotional
goods.
For example, consider the presents you get from
individuals you care about.
about. Consider this: if the item was presented to you as a
gift, it
has already accomplished what it set out to do. Make you
smile. Two
Years later, the present has become an object taking up
room in your house.
since you've never used it and are unlikely to do so. That is
not the case.
going to alter your feelings or the link you have with the
person
Who gave you it? You still value the idea. If, however, the
If this object is merely contributing to the clutter in your
house, you may be better off without it.
If you don't intend to use it, donate it to someone else.
There are three more guidelines you might follow to assist
you with the
The process of decluttering It is a guideline that

minimalists adhere to.
assist them in downsizing their possessions and living a simpler, happier life:
The 10/10 Rule
The 20/20 Rule
The 90/90 Rule
The 10/10 Rule

The Rule of 10/10

Examine everything in your possession. Give it some thought.
idea, followed by the question, "How important is this item to me?" Those
tangible items that you worked so hard for and spent your hard-earned money on.
How much money have you spent, scrimped on, and saved to eventually buy?
How much value does it add to your life? Would you be shocked if I told you?
discover that it is less important than you believe? You might be with the
Materialism is a 10/10 rule.
Here's how it works: grab a pen and paper and jot down the 10.
most costly products purchased in the past decade (10 years).
This includes your automobile, laptop, cell phone, and any other electronic device.
Your house, the jewels you bought List the top ten most costly
big-ticket purchases you made in the previous 10 years. On a separate sheet
Make a fresh list, this time with the ten items that sum up to the
greatest worth and significance into your life. For instance, consider the following:

vacationing with your loved ones or watching your children kid's dancing performance, maybe even a nice supper and catching up

You should have a session with your parents. Take a look at the two lists you've made.

They most likely have nothing in common. Which list is the best?

Are you happier? If it's the latter, it's possible that you won't.

You don't need as much as you anticipated.

The 20/20 Rule

The first rule will remove the need for you to grasp onto anything.

Things under the "just in case I might need them" category The notion that you may need to save your belongings in case of an emergency

Is there ever a time in the distant, hypothetical future when you could use it?

This is how too much clutter develops. It's time to say goodbye to

These things, as well as the 20/20 rule, are where you should start. Begin by acquiring

Get rid of any "just in case" products that cost less than $20.

Could simply be replaced in less than 20 minutes. That way, if you ever come across

You find yourself in a situation where you need one of them "just in case."

products, you can simply replace them for less than $20 in under 30 minutes.

Minutes cost $20. Most likely, you won't miss or use all of the "just in case" items.

In case" stuff you've been hoarding and won't need to Replace them completely.

The 90/90 Rule

When we come face to face with all of your belongings, deciding on the spur of the moment which products are valuable and which are not.
It gets almost impossible. Simplifying your life may not be as simple as you think.
It's as simple as it sounds. Don't be surprised if you find yourself in this situation.
stuck even before you've had a chance to begin properly, especially
when you're confronted with a massive pile of your possessions.
You must begin sifting through. Then, letting go becomes a virtually impossible task.
difficult job because how do you determine what to get rid of?
And what should you keep?
Applying the 90/90 rule. Choose a few objects to begin with and arrange them.
They are there in front of you. Now choose something. It may be whatever you want.
It makes no difference what it is, as long as you choose anything. Once
After you've done that, consider the last time you utilized this. Was it
during the last 90 days? If the answer is no, consider whether you are
I want to put it to use within the next 90 days. If the response remains no, then
Allow it to go. The 90/90-day rule is just meant to be a guideline.
You are not required to follow those figures if they don't work.
in your honor. It may be a 60/60 rule or even a 120/120-day rule.
rule.

Cleaning Up Your Home Office

A nice, organized, and tidy workspace is not always a good thing.

It is not a must for outstanding work or amazing ideas, but it does assist.

a distraction-free workstation with everything you need need within easy reach. When you're in a hurry to meet a deadline,

When racing the clock, a clean and well-organized desk may be a godsend.

and less of a source of worry. We are unaware of how quickly time passes.

spent hunting for stuff. How much time do you devote to planning?

and rearranging items in your home or business workspace When do you feel like things are getting out of hand? The more you possess, the better.

the more time you waste on pointless housekeeping as well as cleaning. The time that might have been spent working on whatever

You have to. Things take up more of our time than we think. Want

to boost productivity? It is a good idea to declutter your desk.

starting point:

Determine What You Want from Your Desk: What do you want from your desk?

What do you see when you think of the ideal work desk? Is it

efficient? Clean? Is everything easily accessible? An unoccupied desk

It adheres to a basic notion using nothing more than a phone, laptop, and a notebook and pen? Your ideal

The desk is probably not as sloppy as it is today, and When you know what you want, it's simpler to strive for it. Remove everything that does not add to the vision.

Return What You Borrow: You may need to do this on occasion.

Take a tip or two from your coworker in the adjacent cubicle.

Instead of abandoning it, return it as soon as you are finished.

putting it on your desk and stating, "I'll get to it later." Later, it might be full.

There are many diversions and other activities that you neglect.

Returning the thing entirely, and guess what? That is called clutter.

You do not need it on your desk. Your new behavior must be

As quickly as possible, return anything that does not belong to you.

If you have no urgent intentions to utilize it, you are through with it.

quite shortly.

Tossing trash—bits and pieces of crumpled paper, etc. brochures, sticky notes, and maybe lunch wrappers.

You had it earlier but didn't have time to throw it away.

Toss everything that is trash and not required for work. out immediately. Recycle anything that can be recycled.

Make it a habit to throw away anything you find.

Not required. This seems to be a straightforward step, but unless you

You're not fully aware of how to tidy your desk.

How much have your routines made you indifferent to the little details?

All the bits and pieces of worthless objects that gather on your tables

Group similar items together. Use the same idea that you do at home and designate a "home of" to everything on your desk.

on its own. "Everything should have a place to call home,

and if it doesn't, it should.
Reconsider if you need it and whether it belongs on your desk.
For example, organize your pens in one container.
Put comparable file folders together, and then put your paper clips in another.
container for them, as well as your other office supplies.
another container. When sorting, the same rule applies.
Clear out your desk drawers. Drawer dividers and separators are available.
excellent at keeping things nice, tidy, and organized.
Create an Efficient Filing System: Consider your options before filing.
When it comes to piles, it's a good idea to ponder before you pile.
I'm working on creating an effective filing system. Much of what we
end up filing is unlikely to be utilized again, and if, while your
During the clearing process, you may stumble across files that you had forgotten about.
There's a strong chance you won't need it anytime soon.
soon. If you still believe you may but don't want to retain the
hardcopy, store it in the cloud, and destroy the remainder.
Reduce the amount of clutter on your desk. What is still on your desk?
Drawers should only contain goods that you want to use. regularly and several times.
Items for Daily Utilization: Only keep on your desk what you want to utilize.
On a daily basis. These are the only things you'll ever need.
Finish your task. Make it after you're through with it.
a practice of putting things away right away before moving on to
the following job.

Keep Personal Items to a Minimum: Keep personal items to a minimum.

goods in order to increase productivity. Personal belongings may be

look nice on your desk, but they are a distraction whether you are working or not.

Whether you recognize it or not, Remember that the brain processes and absorbs information.

more than we understand, and it is always at work in the Even when we're not paying attention, there's something going on in the background. If necessary,

Limit yourself to one personal item on your desk.

Tidy the Cables: Having a bunch of cables all over the place is not a good thing.

It is pleasing to the eye. If feasible, use wifi, but if not,

If you can't, try grouping your cords together using elastic bands.

bands or binding clips to make a clean pile instead of being scattered.

littered throughout the area. At the very least, they will not be in the way.

You run the danger of becoming entangled in something else while you're working.

I'm in a hurry.

Ditching Duplicates: If you have many things that are duplicates,

You don't need the duplicates, so get rid of them. You do not.

Multiples of the same pen or stapler are required. You do not need

duplication of notes or material that is already in digital form.

Before you pick up your luggage and go, clean it.

go out the door, clean your desk, and go through your drawers.

for any residual rubbish you may have overlooked while in

In a rush throughout the day. Nothing is scarier than walking into a

the workplace the following day, already worried by the

The task you see in front of you is from yesterday.

Spend 5 to 10 minutes at the end of the day simply relaxing.

Clearing stuff away will make you feel a lot better.

Changing Your Environment to Change Your Mindset

There is sufficient study and science to demonstrate this.

There is unquestionably a correlation between the physical clutter we acquire and the

adverse effects that come as a direct consequence of such clutter. as in an

a rise in anxiety, increased stress, procrastination, and

Unhappiness and discontent are universal sentiments. However, realizing

What clutter does to you is a fantastic starting point. It is this self-awareness that is important.

That will both encourage you and remind you of why you should put a stop to it.

to it and stop allowing your local surroundings to be

I am surrounded by materialistic pandemonium.

Changing your surroundings alters your perception. Take into consideration

This is the case. You're sitting at your desk, trying to come up with ideas.

ideas. You've been attempting to complete it for the last 30 minutes, but

You're running out of time and feel trapped. Regardless of how hard you try

The mental barrier is preventing you from concentrating your thoughts.

pouring out, so you decide to stand up and stretch your legs.

Take a stroll outdoors to clear your mind. Maybe you'll make a decision.

should bring your laptop and go to a neighboring coffee shop to

Make an effort to get some work done there. When you first come, the aroma of

Coffee floating over your nostrils quickly relaxes you, and You sit down, feeling energetic after ordering your drink, and get straight to work.

to work. The thoughts seem to flow more easily, and before you realize it,

You're almost finished.

Your mentality has an impact on everything you do. No regardless of the scenario or obstacles you are experiencing.

be experiencing in life, the time your thinking transforms is the moment

When will things change? It is ultimately determined by how you see the circumstances.

You can shape the reality around you. Occasionally, the incapacity to strategize

It is not because you lack the ability to generate ideas or solve problems.

ideas. Sometimes it's your immediate surroundings that are the problem.

problem. That is why a change of surroundings makes it seem simpler to get started.

Get your job done and your creative juices flowing again. Altering your

The atmosphere causes you to perceive things in a different light. It goes away.

your thoughts and exposes your thinking to possible inventive ideas

previously hard to think of. You flourish in an environment that

encourages productivity, in addition to the comfort of not having to look at

Here's how altering your surroundings affects your mind:

You Are Aware of Your Resources. It is difficult to recognize what you have to offer.

When you're distracted by the clutter, work with it. A shambles

The setting makes it difficult to think and much more difficult to come up with ideas.

come up with ideas when you are unsure of the resources

You already have. You can at least take a break in a clutter-free environment.

Take a quick glance around and declare, "These are the resources I have."

have," and you may begin working on your ideas based on it.

Those assets.

Material items used to be important to you, but your values begin to shift.

meant so much no longer seem to be so significant when your

The mentality begins to alter. As you make the decision to live a life where

When you learn to live with less, you begin to cherish life more.

Instead of material things, prioritize experiences. As an example, suppose you

respect the time you spend with your family and spouse.

children or friends more than ever before, since

It is obvious that this is what occupies your time. A workstation or environment that

It doesn't matter whether your house is filled with goods; what counts is that you're happy.

You are productive and do your tasks to the best of your abilities.

As "stuff" becomes less important in your life, your perspective will shift.

gradually transition to the point where possessing less is now your norm.

rather than a priority.
You have better time management since there are fewer distractions.
Less time is squandered. You may not have given it much consideration.
how you were spending your time prior to starting decluttering, which made the minutes and hours fly by.
Simply slip by. The more you tidy and begin to see the
The more important you are, the more advantages this method delivers.
Instead, I'm going to focus on things that will benefit me.

Chapter 4: Cleaning Up Your Relationships

Decluttering is not without difficulties, and if you thought minimizing your stuff and cleaning out your workspace was difficult, think again.

Wait till you attempt to clean up your relationships. The most difficult thing will most likely be adapting to not having that connection in your life anymore. Perhaps you need to break connections with someone you've known for years because you've realized their conduct is poisonous and contributing to the stress you already experience. It's still not going to be an easy choice.

You've grown used to their presence, and there will undoubtedly be an emptiness when they're no longer around. It's the same in every relationship you've ever had. When you're accustomed to constantly being around or seeing that individual, their absence will not go unnoticed. Even if you know your choice was the correct one, it might seem lonely at times.

The High Price of Toxic Relationships

A poisonous relationship may happen to anybody, even the brightest and most confident individuals you believed were too clever to make such awful choices. There's no knowing when or how you can end up in a harmful relationship since it doesn't always start out that way. Toxic connections will deceive, injure, and manipulate you, necessitating social cleaning.

We don't give much consideration to decluttering relationships and social minimalism since our attention is generally drawn to the physical component, the things we can see in front of us.

We are visual animals, and it is only when we can see something that it becomes "real." Most of the time, mental, emotional, and even social clutter are an afterthought since we can't see the harm they're causing or how they're affecting us.

"Holding on to a toxic relationship is like drinking poison and expecting the other person to die," Buddha once remarked. When you lose yourself in a toxic relationship, your judgment gets muddled, and it becomes increasingly difficult to discern what is best for yourself. You lose sight of who you are and what you want, and your pleasure becomes secondary. You begin to accept it and create excuses for being in that poisonous relationship because it seems better than having to cope with the agony of letting go of the person you love (or believe you love). Social decluttering is a complex subject. It is easy to get engulfed in a poisonous relationship because they are overwhelming. You lose touch with your own objectives, passions, wants, ambitions, and purpose when you are in toxic relationships. They make you feel helpless and impotent, with no idea what to do next. They increase your tension, fuel your anxieties, and cause worry. Their difficulties start to influence you and become your worries.

After a lengthy period of catering to everyone else's needs

except your own, you grow bitter. To put it simply, the expense of toxic relationships is just not worth it.

How to Clean Up Your Relationships

It is meaningless to be with negative individuals or those that cause you misery. Keeping them around isn't adding value to your life, and it's surely not bringing you pleasure. Negative and poisonous people will only draw you down and lock you at their level, making you as sad and miserable as they are. You don't have to fully detach or dissociate yourself from them (though in certain situations this may be preferable), since it's not always possible. Toxic connections might exist inside your family or among the individuals you work with, making it difficult to avoid them totally. You don't have to ignore them completely, but you should try to spend less time with them and concentrate your energy and attention on more important individuals. Keeping connections because you've known someone for a long time or because you've had a few fantastic experiences with them isn't a good enough reason to keep them if they're pulling you down more than they're lifting you up. People evolve, grow, and develop in a variety of ways. People's connections change as they evolve, and decluttering your social life may require you to learn to let go and be good with it. It will hurt, but hanging on because you feel horrible is a disservice to yourself.

Examining all of your social media accounts This will most likely be the simplest stage in the whole decluttering process. Begin with your social media channels and begin deleting individuals you don't know very well or with whom you no longer connect, as well as those you believe no longer contribute value to your life. It may seem weird at first, but as you delete these "friends" one by one, it will get easier. Don't be concerned about what others will think. Whether those "friends" made little (or no) effort to communicate with you on these social media sites in the past, there's a strong probability they don't care whether you're still linked in the digital arena. Streamline your push notifications by turning off the ones that aren't essential and just retaining the ones that are. Alerts from social networking applications are unnecessary; they just serve to distract you. Alerts should only come from text messages and critical reminders.

Go cold turkey. This will be difficult, but it is the most effective approach to discovering the individuals in your life who actually appreciate your presence and relationship. Stop communicating with everyone and go cold turkey. Now, "everyone" in this context is going to be subjective to how many people you know, so there is no set quantity or quota of individuals you must communicate with.

Avoid being the first to text, the first to call, or the first to make arrangements. Stop cold turkey, sit back, watch, and wait. Observe who notices your "sudden silence" and reaches out to see whether everything is alright. Who are the people who respect your friendship enough to keep it going? Sharing or liking your most recent Facebook status or Instagram post does not qualify. Friendships are valuable when they check in on you at random for no purpose other than to see how you're doing. Or the ones that are there for you when you are at your lowest and darkest. They are the people you can actually rely on in an emergency. You may be astonished to learn that there are many fewer people who appreciate you than you believed. But, at the very least, you're clearing out the superfluous connections while maintaining the ones that give actual worth and satisfaction to your life.

Understanding Your Relationship Values: What kinds of connections are important to you? What kind of connection, in your opinion, brings worth to your life? Is it anything worth investing in? What, more significantly, makes you happy? These are the essential signs to consider while minimizing your social contacts. Always return to a single, straightforward benchmark. Is this connection bringing you joy? Is it contributing to the stress?

Cleaning Up Your Romantic Relationships

Relationships have the potential to endure a lifetime. Something we all desire but don't have
Everyone is fortunate enough to have something to hang onto. Divorce rates in today's society

The world is higher than it has ever been, and clinging on to a
A friendship that is strong enough to endure throughout time
become a valuable commodity. Because love alone is insufficient.
to keep these partnerships going. There must be security as well as a profound understanding.
on an emotional, mental, physical, and spiritual basis. Love requires effort, and if you want to make your job simpler,
You must clear the clutter from your connection. Take away the
Remove the mental, emotional, and spiritual clutter as well as the physical clutter. Any
a negative factor that is putting pressure on your relationship
It must be assessed.
When we are estranged from our companions, we are unaware that
It might be due to clutter (both physical and non-physical). We
don't know how to deal with these feelings of

disconnection, and as a result,
Some individuals use shutting down as a coping method. Instead of collaborating to discover solutions, they isolate themselves from their collaborators.
a solution. Negative tendencies and coping methods continue to exist.
ubiquitous, and unless we deliberately work to simplify our relationships,
It will only become worse, not better.
By completing the following, you may declutter the harmful patterns in your relationship.
following:
Recognizing Patterns: This is a simple initial step.
It is necessary to practice self-awareness. Take note of how you behave.
Take charge of your relationship right now. Do you turn off your computer?
when you're swamped with emotions? Or will you lash out? Do you
Should we collaborate or compete? Conduct a thorough examination.
evaluation of how you and your spouse now deal
Take notice of the negative aspects of stressful or emotional circumstances.
Unhealthy habits of behavior must be altered. Or
In this scenario, it is decluttered.
Nothing pulls people together like negativity.
Nothing beats banding together against a shared foe. In this instance, the
Anything that is impeding your connection is a mutual adversary.
You are preventing yourself and your partner from working successfully together. In the same way that negative
Take, for example, conduct. Consider decluttering a bonding experience.
You and your partner may collaborate on a project. If it has

been a long time,
This might be one since you worked as a team.
Exercise will begin to bring you closer together. in place of
Make it your objective to work against each other on this.
together.
Resentment is a key cause of clutter in any environment.
Anger, resentment, envy, and ego are all components of a
partnership. Everyone
has a sense of ego and pride inside them. How simply these
The extent to which features manifest depends on our
ability to regulate them.
When left uncontrolled, ego can frequently wreck havoc.
Particularly in the relationships that are closest to them.
Ego is
a bad emotion that results in sentiments of resentment
Anger, fear, and jealousy are all emotions. Bringing up
previous disagreements,
Misdemeanors and errors only serve to complicate the
connection.
You're dealing with nothing but toxins. So, let go and let
the past go.
Continue to live in the past.
Learning to Ask: This is a bad habit that generates a lot of
problems.
Clutter in relationships occurs when spouses do not request
what they need.
desire or need. If your requirements are not being satisfied,
you must take action.
ask. Your spouse is not a mind reader, and you should not
expect them to be.
catch up on subtle cues, read your thoughts, or predict your
needs.
Fighting, sadness, and disputes are all caused by thinking.
happen. A lot of communication occurs when assumptions
are made.
Breakdowns are common, and you'll be trying your best to

avoid them.
Your connection will benefit if you learn to speak and ask for what you want.
what you desire.
Expectations Are Clutter: Expectations are another kind of clutter.
Clutter adds no value to your connection. Consider the following scenario:
began each discussion with your companion with the Expectations that something will go poorly. You will most likely
without even trying to undermine the dialogue and make it worse.
because the clutter is unconsciously weighing on you.
your thoughts. Why? because you anticipated things to go wrong.
It takes work to learn to speak with an open mind, but
First, be clear and let go of expectations.

How Can Decluttering Your Home Help You?

Relationships

If there is conflict between you and your family, spouse, or roommate,
The issues in your house may not be totally external. It is possible.
the clutter in your house that causes frequent disputes and simple arguments
annoyance with your spouse, partner, or children's clutter. Clutter causes
We already know that there is disagreement. According to 2016 research,
30% of people who had recently divorced said yes.
One of the primary reasons they split up was the continual butting of heads.
leads the home tasks. This was the third-best answer.

place after drifting apart (35%); and infidelity (35%).
40% of the time.
In the same year, the Pew Research Center performed research.
More than 56% of married people polled said they considered that a good marriage had a lot to do with how the family was run.
The chores were divided. You don't have to go far to find evidence of this.
Clutter also causes discord. Tidying Up, a popular Netflix series
Up with Marie Kondo demonstrates how a cluttered, unorganized home can be transformed.
house and wreck havoc on a couple's relationship.
It's understandable that it's difficult for families and couples to maintain relationships.
today's pristine, clutter-free house without stretching
They stretch themselves too thin, attempting to handle everything. Work, family life, and home management duties, cooking, cleaning, food shopping, washing, and leisure activities
Keeping up with expenses while raising children It's a lot for anybody to handle.
take on, and frustrating if they attempt to do it all on their own.
Decluttering and keeping the home neat may seem low on the priority list.
Priorities of tasks that must be completed, yet something must be completed.
done about it before the cumulative impacts of clutter begin to manifest themselves.
Your physical and emotional health will suffer as a result.
Your house should never be sold.
a state of worry, anxiety, guilt, or overload. You should never do this.
have to be embarrassed or humiliated that someone would

see the
condition of your house.
Aside from boosting your stress levels and being an
eyesore,
How clutter affects your relationships:
Arguing and sniping at each other is hurting your love life.
Being constantly dependent on each other is not a sign of a
healthy relationship. A
A spouse or partner who is concerned by domestic clutter
going to voice their dissatisfaction, be upset, and maybe
resort
Be quickly angered by unpleasant remarks or even name-
calling.
and enraged.
It's Harming Your Children: Assuming you have children,
clutter is harmful to them.
will have a detrimental influence on them by raising their
According to the National Institute of Mental Health,
Health. Making friends is far more difficult for stressed-
out youngsters.
It also causes feelings of loneliness and isolation.
It Isolates You—the discomfort you experience
over your untidy house can crush any ambition you have.
You must invite relatives or friends. Russell Investigations
performed a Rubbermaid survey and found that
People were less inclined to welcome guests if their house
was dirty.
messy. If this has an impact on your relationship, spouse,
or children,
disappointed that they can't invite anybody over because of
you.
It's going to be an issue if you have hoarding tendencies.
It Makes You Feel Exhausted All of the Time—Clutter
may be exhausting.
It was emotionally taxing. Have you ever felt absolutely
depleted?

You're running out of energy at the end of the day, and you're not sure why. You

You don't feel like you've done anything, yet you're fatigued by the

At the end of the day. Clutter has that effect on you. It steals your energy unintentionally because the external

Even when you don't realize it, stimuli are still altering your brain.

just like we discussed in previous chapters.

Relationships are as important as any other area of your life.

You must look after these connections, invest in them, and maintain them.

Work to maintain the connection. Relationships that are happy do not exist.

not happen by chance, particularly when there is more neglect than

There is a process of nurturing going on. If you desire stronger connections, not simply in your personal life, home life, but you must foster every connection you have.

it. Reduce your time spent on consumerism, and you will have more time.

It's time to channel that enthusiasm toward cleaning your surroundings. When

When you simplify your house, the following occurs in your relationships:

You're happier when things don't get in your way.

At the end of the day, they're simply things, and the last thing you want is

allowing anything to come between your relationship. It's not worth it.

Arguing and fussing about clutter spreads bad energy.

In comparison to many other issues you may face,

Clutter is one argument that may be easily avoided if

There was less emphasis put on your possessions. The

Relationships with the people you care about will always

exist.

Any amount of good will always win.

Your Communication Improves: Talking to your

give frequent updates to your partner or spouse on your decluttering progress.

Intervals may strengthen your relationship. Communicating being truthful about what you want and expect

Respect for one another is shown. With fewer things in the house

It's easy to spend quality time together when there's nothing to distract you.

Increasing the strength of your friendship. The more powerful you are,

The more cohesive you are as a group, the simpler it is to discuss anything.

Your Values Are Revealed: Decluttering will disclose your values.

your ideals, a side of you that your partner or spouse may not understand

had previously had the chance to witness all of the material getting

in the way. By stating your priorities, you make it apparent what your priorities are.

deciding to retain what is important, and the act of Decluttering demonstrates to your partner or spouse that you care.

what they must. You cared about your connection with them.

enough to prefer that over amassing material possessions no longer bring any meaningful value or advantage.

Fewer Expectations: By adopting a minimalist attitude, Your expectations will change. You will no longer be You will no longer be able to prioritize wishing to receive presents.

Maintain the urge to purchase, buy, buy. You will not succeed.

Expect your boyfriend or spouse to continue getting things for you.

anything, since you're now more deliberate about the things you do.

you let into your area. Returning to Chapter 3, where Space was mentioned as being more valuable than everything else. Having fewer

hidden expectations you put on your partner to meet You may have wants or expectations around giving and receiving.

Your relationship will be much happier with

Get the disappointment out of the way. No longer will you be disappointed when

Your companion forgets to bring an anniversary present. No

more feeling unhappy and believing your boyfriend doesn't care.

since it has been a long time since they have returned home and are shocked

I'm going to surprise you with a gift. Things don't matter as much now.

You Grow More Grateful: When you declutter, you become more grateful.

eyes to the truth that possessions can never deliver you the type of long-term happiness that you want.

Your mentality, the delight you will get from your loved ones

starts to give thanks. You are thankful to have a

A companion or spouse who is always available to you You are thankful that you

You can rely on them to be there for you when you need it the most.

You're thankful to have someone to love and share your ups and downs with.

downs in order to make memories. You discover how to Thank individuals for the tiny things they do for you.

You're in a good mood.
You're happy because of their existence in your life.
They're there, and you show your gratitude for having them.
They should be present in your life, and this does not just apply to your spouse.
either. This positivism rubs off on others, and before you know it, you're
bouncing off each other's mutual joy, deepening the bond.
You have an even stronger link. It makes you gentler and more compassionate.
When you are supportive, it makes the people in your life happy.
They are aware that you realize and value what they do for you.
You begin to respect each other more; it is critical to
In this circumstance, appreciate everyone's choice, even if it's not yours.
The choice may not be one with which you agree or are comfortable.
wished for. Trying to persuade everyone to accept your clutter
When they are not prepared for (or do not desire to undertake) it, their way of life is
There will be a lot of tension and disputes in the relationship. Mutual trust is the foundation of healthy, successful partnerships.
Respect, understanding, and compromise are all virtues. When you no longer have
Allow little inconveniences, such as needless clutter, to obstruct your progress.
When there is less bickering, it is easy to appreciate each other.
way.

Organizing your priorities and eliminating bad habits

Habits
Good practices help keep your house and life clutter-free. Poor habits
and a lack of priorities will keep your house and
relationships in disarray.
I'm caught in the muck zone. Developing the habit of
making new habits
It will not be easy, but it will be well worth the effort.
Wouldn't it be nice to enter through the door at the end of a
hard day and be greeted by
a house you're glad to be back in, as well as a family,
spouse, or relationship
You like coming home to Now that you've determined your
Priority number one is to reduce clutter in your
relationships; here are some suggestions.
Beneficial practices to begin implementing:
Adopt the forgiveness Habit: Forgiveness is one of the
most effective things you might have to help you let go
It is much simpler to develop harmful behaviors. You will
not only ultimately acquire
the capacity to forgive people over time after letting go of
your grudge
ego, but you'll also learn to forgive yourself, which will
reduce the
You have emotional junk that you carry with you. You will
discover
acceptance, and you'll discover how to be a lot happier
when you do.
Allow yourself to release all of your wrath. Gandhi once
stated:
because "forgiveness is something attributed to the strong."
He was correct.
Make time to breathe and meditate; clear your thoughts.

through promoting simplicity and serenity. Remove yourself from the situation.

load of negativity by developing the practice of scheduling frequent

It's time for meditation and breathing. Mindfulness is really important.

important in this scenario since it assists you in developing the habit of living in the

moment and reduce overthinking, which creates a lot of stress.

There is cognitive fog and clutter. Living in the moment means savoring the present.

Small things that happen to you as they happen The small

For far too long, we have taken some things for granted.

More gratitude and appreciation—there is no substitute for it.

You have a limit to how much thankfulness and appreciation you can convey. Do everything.

every day since it instills in your mind thoughts of optimism and happiness. It is always preferable to allow people in.

rather than feeling the additional love and gratitude in your life.

underappreciated. Simple gestures, thank-you cards, and even

Throughout the day, text messages were delivered informing them of how

How much you value them may have a tremendous impact on

Someone else's day

Only invest in meaningful relationships. Your time is valuable.

Now it's time to make it a habit to keep track of your time.

Moving ahead, invest in the proper connections. Family,

There is no tie between friends, lovers, spouses, or colleagues.

should deplete your vitality and clog your energy. Your
Because you are changing, your relationships will develop
over time.
As a human, you are changing. Mentally, you're evolving
and maturing.
mentally, emotionally, and spiritually. Every connection
you have in your life
should be one that makes you a better person by lifting you
up.
If it doesn't, it's considered clutter.
The Empathy Habit: It takes two to tango.
Interpersonal work, as well as other people's sentiments and
emotions
They are just as important as yours. Begin honing your
abilities to
empathize, to be able to put oneself in the shoes of another
and view things through their eyes. The ability to
comprehend where they're coming from and how they're
feeling.
is going to improve your capacity to interact with them on a
more personal level.
much deeper level than you could before. That is going to
happen.
do wonders for boosting communication in the workplace.
your connection since you can now see things.
another person's viewpoint.
It's acceptable to walk away from something. It's acceptable
to make the decision to walk away from something.
When necessary, make an unpleasant condition a habit.
Especially if done by
You will just aggravate the situation if you walk away.
worse. Take a break and return to the problem with a fresh
perspective.
better solution. It is easy to get overwhelmed by your
emotions if
You're not being cautious. As much as you desire to settle

disputes,
Sometimes the best option is to just walk away.
If you need to go away from the circumstances to clear your mind,
You're letting your emotions get the better of you. If it's going to happen,
maintain your connection and clear the toxicity from your life.
life by learning to move away when necessary.
Being mindful and present with your partner
In terms of your romantic connections, they might benefit from
Making mindfulness a habit Being aware and present enhances your awareness of what is going on in the world.
relationship. Your spouse, like you, is giving it their all in the workplace.
relationship. Based on their knowledge, they are trying their best.
on their experiences and what they've gone through in life thus far.
Nobody would deliberately misbehave. This is exactly what
You must be careful of this since it is easy to forget when
You're irritated, and your thoughts are muddled by clutter. It
It doesn't help that the human brain is geared to concentrate on something right away.
Before evaluating the positive elements, evaluate the negative aspects first. That
explains why defects and imperfections often seem more noticeable and stick out.
out in our memories a lot more than your partner's positive acts.
does.
Being mindful and present allows you to be more adaptable, and learning to
Being adaptable is a key step in creating a healthier, more

sustainable society.

good style of thinking since otherwise it would be impossible.

and irritating to overcome roadblocks when things may not go as planned.

be heading in your direction. You can't control everything, particularly when it comes to the environment.

When it comes to relationships, learning to be adaptable is how you survive.

with the ups and downs and trials that life throws at you. Being

Being adaptable is how you learn to work better with your spouse.

The way it should be: as a team.

You, your partner, and two others are attempting to collaborate to

Make the relationship function. Two distinct individuals with very different

personalities attempting to get along, support, and love each other. Being aware of these variances and the little details

Things you do for each other make it simpler to avoid allowing emotions to enter.

the way and impair your judgment. Be aware, pass less judgment, and listen more.

more. We are not actively listening when we critique our companions.

enough. Judgment already mentally prevents you from being present.

compassionate toward them. This is particularly true when a

When you disagree with what your spouse is saying, you have an argument.

You pass judgment on them because of that. Learn to declutter as part of your decluttering process.

Take a step back and actively listen to what they're saying.

Look for the truth in what they say. Practicing mindfulness in relation to the

The words you choose and the tone in which you express them may have an impact.

protect you from a lot of harmful statements and interactions.

about, and it allows for more positive discussion to take place.

take occur. Your relationship will be happier as a result.

Chapter 5: Cleaning Up Your Thoughts

What would you say is your most valuable resource if you were to name it?

What will the response be? Would you say time is your answer? It seems that time has passed.

It's never enough, yet time is continuous and unchanging. On any given day, you don't have more or less of it. We only have 24 hours a day.

That's all there is to it. There is nothing more or less. residing in

It is not time that is scarce in the information age that we live in today.

Our attention span is a valuable resource. Since the advent of the internet,

The quantity of information we get has grown. dramatically. The issue is that the amount of information we can collect is limited.

At each given moment, the procedure stays the same. As a consequence, we are confronted with

with information overload, an issue that has been developing in recent years.

since the internet began to take off. The more popular the internet grows,

and the more we rely on technology, the more overburdened our brains get. become.

Information is addicting, and we can't seem to get enough of it.

even when we're already taking on more than we're capable of. Just

Consider how many hours we waste idly looking around social media.

Social media is collecting updates, status shares, likes, and comments.

photos and videos. It's a lot to digest for a brain that can't accomplish anything.

well under multitasking strain. Taking in and processing Information is getting harder to obtain, as seen by today's Particularly in business settings. According to one Pew Research Center research

The research center found that in an already crowded environment,

20% of American respondents said they were overworked by

the quantity of information they get. Nonetheless, 77% of those

Respondents said they valued having a lot of information at their fingertips.

67% believe that having a lot of knowledge helps to simplify

their very existence. Americans, it turns out, are rather content.

self-assured in their capacity to deal with the constant flood of information.

They are given.

Being able to cope, however, does not imply that this is beneficial to the

brain. Clutter exists for a purpose, and if we continue to disregard it, it will get worse.

Anxiety, worry, overthinking, negativity, and other subtle symptoms of its existence

Depression) will continue until you put a stop to it. Not Everyone processes data in the same manner, and if you're one of them,

Those who are often worried by how much you have to take, it's

an indication that you've taken on more than you can manage.

It's time to take a breather and declutter.

Is information overload a serious problem?

Information overload occurs when the brain begins to take in more information than it can keep up with and comprehend. In

In 2010, Google decided to count what they thought was every available book on the planet. They arrived at the astonishing figure of 129,864,880 volumes. That was back in 2010. A decade later, that figure has more than certainly quadrupled.

We get more information in a single day than, say, someone from the 1600s, 1700s, or 1800s received in a lifetime. Google's current estimate of the number of existing web pages is in the trillions. Trillions. According to blogging statistics, roughly 70 million new posts are published on WordPress each month. Is it any surprise, therefore, that information overload has become a widespread issue?

It is not an issue to have a lot of information available online. It is not an issue that individuals continue to upload information to the internet. The issue is that we get so inundated with everything we read, watch, listen to, and digest that it becomes more and more impossible to separate excellent information from the throng. The knowledge that enhances and helps your life

Half-baked articles and postings abound online, and most of the time, if something doesn't capture our attention for a long enough period of time, we pass it over or don't bother reading it at all. Only when something catches your attention do you want to stop and eat it out of curiosity. More than that, you feel compelled to devour it. That is the issue.

Whatever the area of interest, there are hundreds of other websites or blogs presenting the same thing. This excludes social media material, forums, and other venues that may be discussing the subject you're interested in. The difficulty is that the quantity of material available on a particular topic of interest might be massive. When you feel like you want to devour everything and learn all you can about a topic but don't have the time to do it, you get overworked. Overloaded.

Overwhelmed by the amount of junk that has accumulated in your head as a result of your inability to digest it fast enough.

Overloading on information is more than simply an issue. It's a plague with no cure, considering how dependent our lives have grown on it. The only way to mitigate its influence on us is through self-control and a few excellent methods to clean your mind anytime you feel there is too much information flooding in at once.

Why do we have information overload?

For one thing, we can credit broad internet access for a huge rise in the volume of information available.

With everything available with a fast Google search, it's difficult not to get engulfed in a sea of information as soon as you log in to any device. Because information can be freely replicated for free, anybody with internet access and the necessary abilities may share information online, providing even more information. We must keep in mind that all of this internet material is just a tiny portion of what we are exposed to on a daily basis. The sights, scents, sounds, and tastes we experience; the emotions we experience; the words we read; the body language cues we take up from others; and even the conversations we have All of this is still information being processed and absorbed by the brain.

Information overload is not good for your brain or memory. Overload, as we have learned, causes mental barriers and, in some cases, a total shutdown, particularly when the brain is confronted with increasingly complicated information that demands more processing time. When the brain is under stress, it may freeze and panic, causing it to stop dead in its tracks. When this occurs, we lose our capacity to think clearly; our minds often go "blank" (as you have no doubt experienced on more than one occasion), and we begin to feel overwhelmed.

Clearly, information overload is much more problematic than we previously imagined.

Other elements that may contribute to this unfavorable overload include:

Too Many Options: Remember the "Paradox of Choice" that we discussed in Chapter 3? Choices are wonderful, but as it turns out, too much of a good thing may be harmful. With so many possibilities and no clue which one to choose, you may feel tugged in a million different ways, making it even more difficult to focus and pay attention.

Emails: An often-overlooked contribution to the mental clutter caused by information, the emails that overwhelm our inbox every day are a significant component of the mental congestion we experience. It doesn't help that more than half of the email content you get is either spam or not significant enough to spend time on. According to Phil Chambers, author of Brilliant Speed Reading, research estimates that around 247 billion emails are exchanged globally every day, with 81% of them being spam. That is a significant amount of data that is sent through email.

Let's face it: social media is here to stay. We have far too many social media channels. Facebook, Instagram, Twitter, Snap Chat, Pinterest, and other social media platforms consume far too much of our time as we browse and seek with no real purpose or meaning. You tell yourself you'll just check these social media applications for a few minutes, but before you know it, half an hour has passed and you've fallen behind on work you should have begun. Not to mention the useless junk you've now accumulated in your thoughts. Social media seldom provides any valuable material.

News: Today's media is relentless in its transmission. But we can't stop ourselves. The desire to understand what is going on is too strong to resist. With shorter attention spans and a continual desire for "new" and "latest" information, news networks are simply feeding into this need with their short news cycles and virtually 24/7 content release.

Information overload is never a good thing.

We spend so much time worrying, overthinking, and overanalyzing that we don't have time to take a step back and examine how information overload affects us and aggravates our anxieties. We respond to what life throws at us rather than considering what is best for us. We didn't have time-saving tools and technology to make it a bit simpler to manage daily life a few years ago, but people were probably less stressed than we are now. The one benefit they did have back then was that they were not bombarded with alternatives and information practically every minute of the day.

When information overload prevents you from taking action, it is a problem. The flow of knowledge is unending, and you'll never be able to keep up quickly enough to take it all in, and the tension generated indirectly from trying to keep up with everything will just wear you down. Even when you're overburdened, the desire to delay is greater than ever since it's difficult to think properly or remain focused on what you need to accomplish.

One route that leads straight to sloth is procrastination. Other bad side effects you may encounter if your brain is overworked and overloaded to the point that you can't think clearly include:

Reduced Motivation: Motivation is the drive that propels us through things we would otherwise avoid. When there is a lack of desire or inspiration to accomplish anything, the door is opened for procrastination to sneak in.

As your desire wanes, the temptation to squander even more valuable time aimlessly scrolling through material that doesn't assist you (such as stuff from social media) grows.

You Remain Trapped in a Negative Mindset: An overburdened brain will find it difficult to break free from the cycle of negativity. That's because being negative is always the easy choice; being positive requires a lot more work. The risk with most of the material we consume is that there is more bad stuff out there, making it simple for our brains to grasp on to it rapidly. Because the brain is predisposed toward negativity bias, which means that it seeks out bad information first before anything else, negative material will always be the first thing that captures your attention.

Your Credibility May Be Jeopardized: Another possible issue created by information overload is the prospect that our credibility may be jeopardized if we don't know how to distinguish accurate and beneficial information from meaningless drivel.

The risk of relying on incorrect information might have major consequences for your credibility and reputation among your peers and those with whom you must collaborate.

Your reputation is one of the most significant assets you may have, and the minute people lose trust in you, your prospects for success shrink even more. A negative impression is difficult to overcome.

You Turn Into a Liability: Having your credibility harmed will result in the second effect of information overload. There is no employer who will consider someone who may transmit inaccurate or misleading information to be of value to the organization. If the information you disseminate is untrustworthy, you become a liability. Your perception shifts negatively. It's difficult not to be skewed toward the negative when you're exposed to more bad news than positive. Our brain believes what we constantly reinforce, and sadly, there is very little "clutter" in the brain that is beneficial. It wouldn't be termed clutter if it were beneficial in the first place.

Your Focus Is Impaired: Another typical issue caused by information overload is daydreaming and a lack of focus, which are exacerbated when the pings and beeps of our mobile gadgets quickly move our attention away and threaten to distract us.

Putting an End to It

The best way to avoid information overload is to restrict the amount of information you consume. Content-control. With so much information bombarding us every day, it is unavoidable that errors will be made along the way. According to Griffiths and Costi (2011), 53% of individuals feel that less than half of the information they get has any genuine value, and 42% utilize incorrect information at least once a week. We obviously need to learn what to skip when confronted with fresh material. Focus on excellent Prioritize excellent information above quantity. Sending a brief and succinct email that goes directly to the point, for example, is preferable to a long-winded email full of superfluous fillers and a roundabout way of getting to the goal. If you must subscribe to newsletters, please do so from reputable sources. They are the ones that have trustworthy knowledge that can help you improve your life, make decisions, and actively contribute to your objectives. The same is true for the news sites you read.

Only watch one or two trustworthy news stations and ignore the others. Choose quality above quantity, and your brain will thank you.

Not Everyone's Advice Is Correct Friends, relatives, and colleagues may suggest or tell you what you "should" read or listen to. They discovered that information.

They believe it will be beneficial to you and are informing you. It's wonderful that they're attempting to assist, but keep in mind that not everyone's advice is necessarily your own. This implies that just because it was the perfect kind of information for them doesn't guarantee it would benefit or educate you in the same manner. If you attempt to eat everything that anybody you know suggests, you'll quickly get mentally exhausted as you try to keep up with it all. Limit your information by limiting your material and concentrating on trustworthy or dependable sources.

Be Extremely Picky: Knowing what to skip will become second nature as you develop the habit of being very careful about the stuff you allow your mind to receive. This is one method of reducing information overload. The information you consume should serve a purpose. That purpose might be related to a goal, strategy, or task you are working on. If the knowledge you're absorbing has nothing to do with any of these, you probably don't need it. You don't need it if it's not knowledge you're going to integrate or act on right away. You don't need anything if it isn't going to affect your choices or actions. You don't need it if it isn't helping you reinforce, point out, or solve an issue. Consume just what you can use right now and leave everything else as an afterthought.

The Magic Number of 3: If you often seek material for a particular goal, for example, if you're a new company owner looking for as many resources as possible to help you get started, you should restrict your number of sources to three. It might be tempting to consume and seize as much free material as possible, but this may not be the best strategy. You must keep in mind that all of these distinct sources may provide contradictory information. When you don't know which advice to follow, it might be perplexing and generate mental clutter. What is the best advice? Limit your trusted, dependable sources to three and concentrate on them. If you have some free time and don't feel overburdened, consider going around and seeing what additional information is available. Take advice from a source who is your cup of tea.

Don't multitask. Trying to accomplish two things at once is inefficient. In reality, you're exacerbating the issue of information overload by doing so. Multitasking "forces" your brain to become confused. Should you respond to the SMS that just came up on your phone or the email that you were halfway through typing? Should you complete your proposal first or start working on a new duty your employer just assigned you? Multitasking is not for everyone, and just because someone you know does it doesn't guarantee it will be as successful for you as it is for them. If multitasking just makes you feel more overwhelmed than ever, then what you're doing is counterproductive rather than productive. If this way of working isn't a good match for you, concentrate on one project at a time and finish it before moving on to the next if you want to be more productive.

Take a Break: We all need breaks during the day to replenish our batteries before we entirely exhaust ourselves.

The internet has a way of hooking you and keeping you wanting more.

You binge-watch for hours on Netflix and YouTube, devouring more than you can handle. The internet will not remind you to take a rest. You must select when to do so. When it becomes tough to concentrate or pay attention, your brain needs a break from all the information it has been digesting all day. It is OK to take pauses without feeling bad about them. If you need a break, take it and return rejuvenated and ready to be more productive in the next few hours.

Stop being distracted by social media as well.

How often do you halt or abandon a task midway through the day because you become distracted? Maybe a coworker stopped by for a quick conversation, or maybe a handful of buddies texted you and you couldn't wait to respond. Perhaps you couldn't resist the impulse to check in on social media or watch a YouTube video or two.

Diversions are omnipresent, and social media is the leading source of everyday diversions. Social media increases the amount of clutter in your brain by intensifying the emotions that you experience. Certain information has the ability to accomplish this, but since we are not actively aware of it, it's easy to miss the connection and realize social media might be directly adding to the clutter in our minds.

Social media functions in subtle ways. The photographs, memes, shared material, and rare amusing videos may seem lighter and entertaining, but here is where the risk lies. It distracts us from the useless junk we're consuming. Asking anyone to explore social media is risky.

Going a whole day without checking their social media accounts is akin to asking an addict to quit cold turkey. It is not without difficulties. It is not impossible, but it is incredibly tough. However, this tremendous source of clutter must be removed.

Streamlining: Reduce the number of push notifications

you get by turning off the ones that aren't essential and just retaining the ones that are. Notifications from social networking applications are unnecessary and just serve to distract you. Text messages and urgent reminders should be the only sources of notifications. You don't need your phone to flash every 5 minutes to inform you who liked your picture or status, or who just shared your material. These are both unneeded and unimportant. Return to Chapter 2 and the Eisenhower Matrix. If they are not urgent or vital, they may wait until the end of the day after you have finished everything else.

Organizing Your Phone's Apps: Would it surprise you to learn that having a single page for all of your applications is quite feasible? Begin by looking through your existing applications and eliminating anything you no longer want or wish to use.

Your home screen should only include applications that are really important to you and those you use regularly every day. Some may find it difficult to erase the applications on their phone, and it may seem strange at first to have your phone screen appear startlingly empty and deserted. However, as you get accustomed to the ease of use, you'll wonder why you didn't do it sooner because of how much simpler it has made navigating through your cell phone. Consider cleansing your contact list as well, eliminating any numbers you no longer need. The most significant numbers will always be those of your family and friends, and when it comes down to it, that's all you need.

Cleaning Up Your Social Circles: Unfollow groups and pages on Facebook that you are no longer interested in, particularly if they are no longer relevant to you. Remember that social media should only be used to stay in contact with individuals, as well as businesses or organizations in whom you have a real interest or care.

Connect Only with People You Know: If you don't instantly recognize someone on social media, consider declining their friend request. You don't need 500 individuals on your friend's list if they aren't people that matter to you.

Quality over quantity is something you can apply to your social network as well. Having just 10 high-quality connections on social media is preferable to having 100 contacts that are unimportant to you.

Final Thoughts and Digital Decluttering Advice

When you think about it, it's remarkable how much of your life can be simplified. You may be wondering why there is a need for digital cleaning. Why would you need to declutter your computer, for example, if it seems to be running just great right now?

Computers, like the rest of our lives, need decluttering since having too many items saved on them can progressively slow them down. Not to mention how too much junk will leave you with very little capacity to keep your data if you do not clear up your system on a regular basis. A digital cleanliness regimen may be just as helpful as a physical cleanup routine. Clutter on your digital devices may not be as obvious or apparent as clutter in your physical surroundings, but that doesn't imply it doesn't exist. The clutter will still be there, piling up file after file, document after document, and we won't even notice it until we start wondering why our gadgets aren't operating as well as they should.

Digital decluttering may lead to increased productivity, and since we depend so heavily on our many devices and gadgets in our contemporary world, it's critical that they work for us rather than against us.

Computers, laptops, mobile phones, tablets, and even smartwatches were meant to simplify our lives and make things simpler so we could spend less time on our jobs, but the reverse has happened. All of the additional "hours" you were meant to gain from speedier internet processing have now been spent sifting through mounds of emails that need to be sorted out, looking for papers online, and, of course, endless hours spent idly surfing around social media applications.

It's time to disconnect and delete all of your old internet accounts. You've undoubtedly signed up for hundreds of internet services and accounts, some of which you've long forgotten about yet continue to get emails from. Why retain such accounts if you can't even remember your login information and password?

Streamline your online life by getting rid of everything that isn't absolutely required. Simplify your thinking and your digital life by doing the following:

Clearing Out Your Inbox: Consider limiting yourself to just one email account. Or two, if you wish to keep your professional and personal email addresses distinct. How many email accounts do you now have in addition to the one you need for work? There is no need to have Gmail, Yahoo Mail, or Hotmail all at the same time; there is no actual necessity for numerous email accounts. Choose one email address to work with and delete the others.

Unsubscribing from Annoying and Ineffective Emails Examine your email content and unsubscribe from communications that no longer interest you. Emails that are not relevant, valuable, or have a significant influence on your life should be deleted. All of those subscription emails alerting you to the newest deals and sales are useless diversions that clutter up your inbox.

Checking it Twice (Personal Emails): Once in the morning and once in the evening Unless you anticipate something crucial to arrive throughout the day. Aim to answer and catch up on emails in no more than an hour. Work emails should be maintained solely during work hours, and everything else that happens after hours should be postponed until tomorrow unless it is exceedingly and completely critical. We're talking about a sense of urgency, as if your career is on the line. If it isn't, emails aren't a priority and can wait.

Turn Off Email Alerts: Turn off your personal email alerts; you don't need them on all day.

Controlling the number of emails you get every day can drastically reduce your screen time. You only need to check your personal emails twice a day (once in the morning and once at night), and once you've removed and unsubscribed from the unnecessary newsletters and "spam" content, you won't need to check your inbox as frequently (unless, once again, you're expecting something urgent). Work emails are a little more complicated. Still, you may declutter by turning off your email notification pop-ups when you need to focus on a task. When you're through with what you're doing, check your email to see if anything else has arrived. Having those pop-up alerts might be immensely distracting while you're attempting to enter something crucial. At the same time, it's not fully viable to dodge work emails entirely during work hours. As a result, the ideal middle-ground method is to deactivate the pop-up notifications and only check after you've completed your tasks.

Conclusion

Thank you for reading all the way through Declutter Your Mind; we hope it was educational and provided you with all of the skills you need to reach your objectives, whatever they may be.

It's almost like peeling an onion when it comes to mental cleaning. To get to the interior bulb of the onion, you must peel away the layers. Decluttering the mind has the same effect. You're gradually going through the process of peeling back every harmful notion you have (with the aid of the instructions in this book) until all you're left with are the realities you need. If we took the same care and focused on our thoughts as we do with our bodies, life would be quite different. We spend a lot of time worrying about how we appear, the clothing we wear, and the food we eat. What if we began doing the same for our minds?

Mind decluttering. When you can identify what matters most, it allows for a lot more self-love and thankfulness. Your family and friends. Family and friends. Relationships. Happiness and health All of those things are already in front of you, and it's only after you've swept away the trash that you can see them again. Peace follows mental clarity. Freedom from superfluous drama, views, and obligations that are not worth expending energy on comes with mental clarity. You can achieve your maximum potential when there are no distractions in your path, much as a vehicle can travel full speed ahead when the route is clear. So, get rid of your negative ideas and restrictive beliefs. You are more competent than you realize.

Finally, if you found this book beneficial in any way, please leave a review on Amazon!